A Passion for Jewelry

A Passion for Jewelry

Secrets to Collecting and Caring for Your Jewelry

Laura Fronty

Photographs by
Yves Duronsoy

RIZZOLI
NEW YORK

CONTENTS

Page 2

*Here I am at four years old
wearing a charm necklace
designed by my grandmother. I
have always kept this memento,
and it remains a source of
inspiration for my own lucky
charm necklaces and bracelets.*

Below

*An attractive way to arrange
earrings. Murano-glass drop
earrings by Dona Giacometti.*

《 *There are no ugly jewels; just jewels that are badly put together and worn poorly.* 》

COCO CHANEL

Portrait of a Young Girl with Jewelry

I have always been surrounded by jewelry, having grown up with an eccentric and creative woman who considered jewels to be her second nature. She never left home without donning her earrings and rings. To celebrate my birth, she designed a one-of-a-kind necklace: medals, stones, beads, and talismans chosen from the four corners of the earth hung from a silver chain. This necklace is the first piece of jewelry that I can remember.

In our house we also had a collection of theatrical jewelry that was my greatest pleasure. It was displayed on a branch of driftwood attached to the wall. All I had to do was climb onto a chair, reach up, and satisfy every child's greatest wish: to become someone else. I was transformed into the Queen of Sheba wilting under the weight of her gems, a gypsy girl who could predict the future, or an Indian princess draped in a silk sari, silver bracelets tinkling at my wrists.

In the summer, I would become a miniature goddess adorned with necklaces and bracelets. The beach offered me its treasures: surf-polished pebbles and small bits of sea glass colored as beautifully as precious stones. I would gather them carefully in a box whose lid was encrusted with iridescent shells.

In my adolescence, I wandered the flea markets hunting for the earrings of my dreams. I imagined that I could own 365 pairs: one for each day of the year! That is a goal I never achieved, but my passion for jewelry remains intact.

Above all, I love the treasure hunt: plunging my hand into a box and finding a lovely old chain in the inextricable tangle, uncovering a necklace of marbled Venetian glass beads, or a four-leaf clover enclosed in a glass medallion. An orphaned earring will send me off on a frenetic search for its exiled sister. These quests make me every bit as happy as those fantastic jewelers' windows before which I can only dream.

INTRODUCTION

A Short History

People have been making jewels since prehistoric times. Carved, pierced, polished, and fashioned into the shape of beads, the first elements of primitive jewelry consisted of stones, bones, animal teeth, and shells. To adorn his body, ancient man also made use of dried plants that had been tinted and woven, along with leather, feathers, cloth, hair, and fur. Only very rare traces of these early organic jewels have survived, as the fragile materials have decayed over the centuries. We can merely contemplate the splendid ornaments of people from distant lands to give us an idea of what jewelry must have looked like in the time of our ancestors.

Jewels were worn for many reasons, but their primary function was to seek favor. Necklaces, pendants, bracelets, charms, and ear ornaments, tastefully assembled according to shape and color, possessed precise purposes. They served as amulets, magical accessories with protective and ritual uses. This tendency can still be found today as charms and other lucky talismans become in vogue again.

Jewelry also had more utilitarian functions, such as the clasps that served to hold clothes together: we see this in examples of ancient fibulae, hooks, pins, belts, and buttons. Their functions as tools of seduction as well as for providing pure aesthetic pleasures were just as important.

Finally, we must not overlook the significance of jewelry as an investment. Jewels were transportable assets, with a relatively stable value, that could be easily liquidated if necessary.

People have often associated jewelry with superstition, as demonstrated by these jewels from ancient civilizations: pre–Colombian necklace in jadeïte, together with a button from the same material, and an ancient Egyptian eye amulet.

Precious Metals

Gold and Silver

The Splendor of Gold

The passion for gold, object of desire and wonder, has not been eclipsed since man first learned to fashion it for his own ends. More precious than any other metal, it shines with unparalleled brilliance, evocative of the sun, to which it was frequently compared in many ancient civilizations.

No one knows for certain when the first nugget appeared, but we do know that, somewhere around 6000 B.C., man transformed himself into a goldsmith (the French word *orfevre* derives from the Latin roots *aurum* for gold and *faber* for producer). Beginning in ancient times, caravans from the Orient and Asia would accumulate a stockpile of gold in Africa, specifically from West Africa's Gold Coast (which is comprised of today's Ghana and a section of Mali). Traders would exchange other precious goods—spices, incense, ivory, and silk—for the coveted metal.

THE KARAT AS THE UNIT OF MEASUREMENT

The proportion of pure gold in an alloy is expressed in karats (sometimes spelled "carats"). Karats are symbolized by the letter K (or C), which derives from a reference to a particular Byzantine coin called the *solidus*. This coin's weight was the equivalent of 24 *keration* ("horns" in ancient Greek).

In antiquity, goldsmiths used carob seeds to weigh gold. They were shaped like horns, and therefore the word "keration" was designated as the unit of mass used to measure gold. The Arabs transcribed the word as *qirat*, which gives us our contemporary word "carat."

Karats express the number of parts of pure gold contained in the metal out of a total of 24. In its most common form—18 karat—there are 18 parts fine gold out of 24. Today, "karat" designates the fineness of the gold while "carat" is used for measuring gemstones (1 carat equals 0.2 grams).

THE IMPORTANCE OF THE GOLD HALLMARK

The quality of gold is designated by its hallmarks. On a modern jewel, the hallmark is easily legible: a small engraving in the metal in the form of symbols such as an animal, a crown, or a head. In certain countries, such as Spain, the United States, and Canada, the mark is often only the numeric designation of the metal's fineness: 18, 14, or 9 karat.

Hallmarks can be found on the band of a ring, the clasp of a necklace, chain, or bracelet, and the back of an earring. Since 1938, in France, the mark of an eagle's head turned to the right indicates the official guarantee of the French state.

On a piece of jewelry acquired in France, the mark of an owl or a weevil (beetle) indicates that the piece was either previously owned or bought outside of French territory.

Goldsmiths also stamp their work. Well-known jewelers and goldsmiths use their initials or distinctive marks to attribute a piece to their workshop.

While marks on older pieces are often worn down, they can sometimes be identified.

From the Intensity of Pure Gold to the Nuance of Alloys

Pure 24-karat gold has a deep, shimmering yellow color. Some designers are able to achieve this special color by creating "bloomed gold" whereby all the surface colors of the metal alloys are eliminated through a simple chemical process of dipping the gold into an acid bath. 18-karat gold thereby attains the warm appearance of pure gold.

Mixed with other metals, gold takes on other tints. Gold and white are still the most popular, but rose has been attracting more attention in the last few decades.

Yellow gold contains small amounts of silver and hints of copper.

✳ Weighing gold

The value of a jewel is not always measured by its weight. The date when it was created, its rarity, and the craft of the artist who designed it must also be taken into account. An antique piece may be more valuable than a modern piece that weighs more.

Left

Jewels under cover. These creations in white gold by H. Stern are set next to a 22-karat gold antique Indonesian ring.

Right

This Scandinavian vermeil brooch is identifiable from its hallmark and the stamp of the designer. You can also see the lettering on the metal that indicates where the piece was made. Next to the loupe, you can make out an eagle's head marked inside a gold band.

White (or gray) gold can be confused with silver if you don't check the hallmark. When placed side by side, the difference is clear: the tint of the gold tends to be slightly grayer than the silver. White gold is alloyed with silver, nickel, or palladium. It has also sometimes undergone a treatment known as "rhodium plating," which gives it a platinum tint.

Rose gold was very fashionable from the nineteenth to the mid-twentieth century. The proportion of copper alloyed with silver is important to its composition.

Right

Various hallmarks. Connoisseurs are experts at distinguishing these marks, which a novice may not recognize. They can help determine the age and provenance of a jewel.

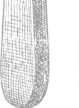

Red gold is a variant of rose gold that contains a slightly higher percentage of copper. Green and blue gold are much rarer and were employed primarily by jewelers during the art nouveau period. They were used to create color contrasts in designs inspired by the natural world.

Green gold is a mix of pure gold, cadmium, and silver that reflects a greenish sparkle.

Blue gold is an alloy with iron that gives it a surprising blue nuance.

✳ Not all that glitters is gold

If there is no hallmark on the metal, it is advisable to use a touchstone or revealing liquid (chemical acids). Rub the metal on a black stone such as slate, then place a drop of acid where the gold has ground off onto the stone. If the mark disappears, it is not gold. Note that the metal could have a lower gold content (less than 18 karats), which might be revealed by dropping a different grade of liquid on the touchstone.

IT LOOKS LIKE GOLD!

Gold has always been imitated. In antiquity, people who were not able to afford pure gold wore jewelry made from bronze, baked clay, or plaster covered with a thin layer of gold.

Vermeil is solid silver with a gold plate. In time, the silver often reappears from underneath the gold, especially when the covering layer is not thick.

Left
This box includes three acid bottles and a touchstone. The bottle contains a blue liquid that will test whether the gold is 18-karat yellow, red, or rose gold.

Right
Common metals may have the appearance of gold when they are plated or gilded like this bronze bracelet and Pomponne ring adorned with pieces of lava and coral.

Following page, left
Jewels created by contemporary jeweler Walid Nakkad, who is refined and unostentatious. Made in gold and fine stones, they radiate a sense of harmony and equilibrium, expressed by the round and spherical shapes.

Following page, right
Infinity bands. One of the most ancient types of jewelry created by mankind, they have great symbolic power. The wedding ring, worn on this finger (the "ring finger") on the left hand, symbolizes eternal love.

In France during the eighteenth century, two goldsmiths developed an alloy with a base of copper and zinc. Louis XV granted them the privilege of using the royal Hotel de Pomponne in Paris as their workshop, and the alloy derived its name from this royal abode.

Around the same time in England, Christopher Pinchbeck also discovered the virtues of the identical alloy, which was bestowed with his name in England. Today, Pinchbeck or Pomponne jewelry is highly prized in the antiques market.

Imitation (or costume), gold-plated, or gold-lined jewelry—the difference between the latter two types lies in the processes used for fusing the gold to the base metal—can be recognized by the absence of a hallmark. The metal will also fail the touchstone test. Like vermeil, these pieces can be regilded, but unless the piece is a particularly lovely example of late nineteenth- or early twentieth-century work, there is often little interest in pursuing this process.

GOLD AROUND THE WORLD

In France, the gold standard is 18 karat. Whatever its color, this gold must contain 750 grams of pure gold for every one thousand grams of metal.

A lovely Victorian jewel bought in London can be 14 karat or even 9 karat, the lowest standard of gold currently found in Great Britain.

In the United States, unless the piece is stamped with an 18-karat hallmark, most jewelry is made with 14-karat gold. In other places, such as North Africa and

Left

Vermeil jewels successfully pass the test of time, and these three antique objects are proof. This French strand of lily of the valley, the braided Russian bracelet, and the Asian brooch have lost their original gilding, letting the silver show through. If they had been made from gilded metal, they would not have maintained such charm.

Above right

Antique earrings with hinged clasps must be cared for very closely. Over time, the clasp may come loose, and the earring may open without the wearer noticing. With a jeweler's pliers you can lightly and carefully pull back the upper part of the clasp.

Turkey, a lower gold standard is acceptable. Pieces can even be made from a standard as low as 8 karat. This is not a problem as long as you intend to keep the jewelry for yourself. But buyers should be aware that the resale of such items can be tricky in a country such as France where state regulations are very strict. In fact, it used to be illegal to sell substandard gold. Any secondhand or imported jewelry that was not stamped with a hallmark were sent to the French state agency that guarantees the content of gold before it could be resold with a legal gold mark.

✳ Certificates

If you want to buy an 18-karat gold jewel in a country that produces gold of a different fineness, a certificate from the seller will provide you with a guarantee and help avoid unpleasant surprises.

In India, jewelers prefer to use pure 22-karat, or sometimes 24-karat, gold. Nonetheless, even the loveliest of pieces can be made of only the thinnest layer of 22-karat or 24-karat gold leaf over a base of wax or resin.

Egyptians are also fond of 22-karat gold, but they find it so costly that their beads are often hollow and quite fragile. These tempting beads look much like those you can admire in the Museum of Egyptian Antiquities in Cairo. They have been manufactured in the same manner since the time of the Pharaohs. Alas, over the course of time, the lovely string of gold beads you purchased in the Egyptian bazaar may become deformed and dented. Try having the gold beads melted and transformed into a plain gold bangle, as thin as a reed.

Left

These Indian beads hide their secret well. This statuette is adorned in gold, with its Indian necklace of cone-shaped beads. They are actually made by fusing a layer of gold leaf to a wax core. There is also a silver version of these unique beads.

Right

An unusual ring bearer. This little bronze donkey would ordinarily be used as a salt dispenser. Here, gold rings have been substituted for salt—a nice way to use an everyday object to help store your jewelry.

HOW TO BUY ANTIQUE PIECES

Antique and used jewelry can be purchased from antique stores, specialized secondhand dealers, auction houses, and flea markets.

To avoid making a mistake over that lovely piece you may be admiring, buy from a reputable jeweler. It should be easy to obtain a certificate containing a description of the jewelry and the price paid—a handy document if you wish to resell the piece or for insurance purposes if you lose it.

Auction houses sometimes conceal marvels, such as antique jewelry—rings

✳ The indispensable loupe

Before buying a piece of jewelry, examine it in great detail with a loupe. This small accessory allows you to read hallmarks and detect scratches and signs of wear on a chain, a bracelet link, or an earring fastener.

or earrings—made of pure gold or genuinely ancient pieces, but it is always safer to know the rules of this market before you buy.

For example, do not let yourself be drawn into bidding above the price you have set for yourself. Do not believe that you are necessarily getting a bargain, and that the price is lower than it would be at a jeweler's: there is often a reserve price below which the piece cannot be sold.

Once you get to know a seller, you can ask to reserve a piece or to pay for it in installments. Sellers can also teach you to recognize styles, periods, and the individual traits of goldsmiths.

To really form an educated eye that is able to pick out the most interesting jewels, you must take the time to read books written by experts, attend exhibitions, and consult with antique specialists. And yet, as with any kind of collection, it is also important to trust your own instincts.

Left
A jumble of jewelry set before a still life of roses.

Right
A loupe is useful to detect missing pieces, wear and tear, and any hallmarks. In this picture you can see that this Napoleon III medallion has lost a tiny pearl.

Trying on a piece of jewelry is as important as trying on clothes: your complexion and the colors of your eyes and hair can all change your initial, more abstract appreciation of a necklace, bracelet, ring, or earrings.

If you do buy an antique, the weight of the gold should not be your most important consideration. Certain eighteenth- and nineteenth-century jewels are ravishing but very delicate and fragile. What matters most are the qualities of the piece, its relation to a particular style (for example, Directoire, Napoleon III, art nouveau, art deco, or 1940s and 50s), and the craft of the goldsmith.

Do not worry if the gems have been replaced by pieces of colored glass, which was once a popular art itself. An antique jewel is a piece of work that carries traces of the past. However, you may want to dismiss jewels that are too marked by previous use, have a fragile setting, or

✳ Clean and shiny gold

To clean gold, there is nothing better than washing it in a bit of soapy water (handcrafted Marseille soap or dishwashing liquid), then rinsing it with clear water, and polishing it with a soft cloth.

have stones that are pocked or missing. These may be too difficult to restore in the end. Yet, it has become possible, with the use of laser welders, to repair even antique and fragile jewelry decorated with stones. In the past, the heat from the welder would irreparably damage the gold; the piece could only be mended with pewter, not an aesthetically pleasing choice. Time lends gold a patina, just like the sea polishes pebbles, so make sure your antique jewel feels smooth and soft on the skin.

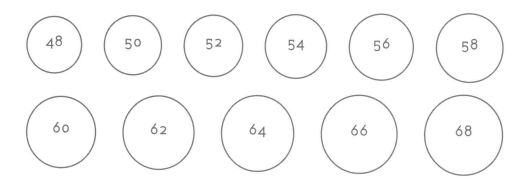

48 = 153 mm	60 = 192 mm
50 = 160 mm	62 = 198 mm
52 = 166 mm	64 = 204 mm
54 = 172 mm	66 = 210 mm
56 = 178 mm	68 = 215 mm
58 = 185 mm	

Above

Rings: each finger thickness corresponds with a size. A jeweler will measure the finger with a finger-ring gauge that will be placed on the appropriate finger to determine its exact size.

Right

When a ring becomes too tight, immerse your finger immediately in cold water and lather it up so that the ring slides off more easily.

✳ Useful advice

Be careful with hollow gold jewelry, which may be less expensive but can be much more fragile. Mixing silver rings and bracelets with gold can cause black marks on the gold when it comes in to contact with the silver.

CARE AND MAINTENANCE

Gold cannot be altered by corrosion, moisture, excessive cold, or natural heat from the sun. Nonetheless, chlorine and bleach are not recommended.

Curiously, gold can become tarnished by the seaside, where the salt air covers it with a thin gray veil. Following the example of our ancestors, it can be cleaned with a soft-bristle brush that has been barely dipped in water and baking soda. Rub the jewel gently with the brush, then rinse, dry, and polish it with a soft cloth. If you prefer a more brilliant shine, polish it again with a cloth lightly dampened with alcohol: the sparkle of your jewel will rival sunlight.

You can also wash gold in water mixed with a drop or two of ammonia, but the smell is not pleasant. You should handle this mixture carefully.

You may also take your gold jewelry to be polished by a professional in order to restore its shine.

A bangle or chain with large links that feels strangely light is probably hollow. Scratches or dents to these pieces are irreparable. If it is only half hollow, the piece will be somewhat more resistant as the gold is thicker.

If your gold jewelry no longer pleases you, it can be taken to a jeweler or a designer who can melt it down and transform it into an original piece that will better suit your taste and style.

Broken or permanently damaged jewelry can also have a second life after it has been melted down.

Carefully examine the posts or hoops on earrings, particularly those that use hinges. These pieces grow fragile with use and can break without warning.

Above left

A pair of large hoops decorated with clovers of fire opal, signed by Marie-Hélène de Taillac. This designer works almost exclusively in pure 24-karat gold. She acquired her passion and skill for designing in gold, without alloys, while working in India.

Right

These signet rings are ornamented with antique intaglios, which were mounted on the bands more recently. The ring showing a man's profile consists of a hollow gold band and is filled with wax or plaster—a common style in antiquity.

Left

The studio of Walid Nakkad. A jeweler's work always begins with a watercolor of the piece that he has designed (here we see a white gold ring, set with diamonds). Next step is creating the mold in wax, and then the jewels are prepared for mounting. Finally, the metal is polished for its final look.

Above

A page torn from a catalog of rings, dating from the beginning of the twentieth century. It shows a marquise setting (upper right), a diamond solitaire, and several engagement rings. Some are "swirl" style while others are set with two different stones—two styles very popular during the period.

The Purity of Silver

Silver symbolizes the moon, its purity, and its white glints. Its name is believed to derive from the Sanskrit word *ar-jun* that means both "white" and "shining." In antiquity, silver was often deemed more valuable than gold. In Egypt, for example, it was considered extremely precious. But unlike gold, which suffers almost no ill effects from age over the centuries, silver is quite fragile and prone to oxidation, causing it to deteriorate. Once the Spanish conquistadors began to exploit the silver mines of the New World, entire ships were needed to carry the metal to Europe and Asia. Today, as then, the majority of the world's silver comes from Latin America.

A SOFT METAL

Silver is too malleable to be used in its pure state. After gold, it is the softest and the most ductile of metals and, like gold, it can be stretched into wire thread. It is alloyed with other metals, most commonly copper, in order to harden it. However, unlike gold, which takes on different hues when alloyed with other metals, solid silver remains white with gray tints.

In antiquity, there was a widely used alloy made from a base of gold and silver. This metal has been forgotten in our time, but its beautiful color—simultaneously pale and glimmering—deserves to be rediscovered by designers.

SILVER AND CUSTOMS

In certain civilizations, silver is preferred to gold. In Africa and Asia, silver is worn daily while gold—which is rarer and more costly—is reserved for urban dwellers or for more ceremonial settings. In these countries, for centuries, metalsmiths have produced magnificent jewelry from silver through the art of chiseling, casting, enamel, or niello. The jewelry was often decorated with symbolic stones—such as coral, cornelian, turquoise, and amber—which serve to protect and bring good luck.

In India, women have always prized silver, and their jewelry reflects this passion. Their silver is cast, then recast, eternally transformed so that over thousands of years women from the middle and lower castes have decorated their arms, wrists, necks, ankles, hair, and clothes with this silver, thus displaying their dowry directly on their bodies.

Left

Floating jewels and sculptures, the netlike pendant (it holds small fish made of enameled silver) and the cuff bracelet are works by Chloé Laderach. She is a jewelry designer who works with silver wires and turns them into valuable mesh.

BELIEFS AND SUPERSTITIONS

In antiquity, newborns were given silver jewelry. The metal was thought to keep away evil spirits and protect the baby while it slept.

In the Maghreb, the Middle East, and Asia, silver is still believed to have protective power; and the Tuaregs of North Africa, for example, don't wear gold because they believe it arouses the attention of the evil eye.

In India, newborns are bedecked in silver anklets decorated with tiny bells. Their cheerful tinkling allows the mother to keep track of her child's movements once the baby learns to crawl.

❋ Nielloware technique

To make niello (from the Latin *nigellus* meaning "blackish") the metal is first engraved, then the indented designs are filled with a black alloy of silver and other metals that have been baked, such as enamel.

Up until the beginning of the twentieth century, similar virtues were attributed to silver in Europe. In Germany, for example, pieces of silver were frequently sewn onto the jackets of young soldiers because they were believed to ward off bullets.

The preference for silver over gold sometimes has its source in religious beliefs. In early Islam, true believers were not allowed to wear either gold or silk during their earthly life lest they be denied these pleasures in paradise. Over time, religious law has relaxed its strictures. In principle, the prohibition still holds for men, but women, at least, are allowed to dress themselves in jewelry made of gold or vermeil.

Left

Pretty chain links come in a wide variety of models with evocative names—such as jaseron chains, fetter chains, coffee bean links, and mariner links—which give the chain or "sautoir" its charm. Here, we see models of chains ornamented with designs and links dating to the beginning of the twentieth century.

Right

To untie knots from chains, clasp them in your hand and pour several drops of cooking oil over them. Rub gently.

Previous pages

A history of hearts: reliquary hearts, perfume bottle hearts, and other types. In this collection, there is even a small bronze heart (on top) dating from antiquity. The heart was one of the symbols favored by the early Christians.

Below left

Small treasures stored in a box, waiting to be cleaned and repaired.

Right

Silver can sometimes take on surprising colors in the hands of a designer (these are by Doris Betz). This is an example of a necklace of tiny black pearls with oxidized silver, strung in the shape of links. The matte silver ring has an engraved niello design, while the flower ring is also made of oxidized silver.

✳ Distinguishing between the real and the fake

Look out for imitations; they do not have the same market value as pure silver.

If you have any doubts about the jewelry, you must apply the touchstone test followed by the revealing liquids (chemical acids). Rub the metal on a black stone such as slate, then place a drop of acid on the spot that the silver has marked. If the mark disappears, it is not silver.

SILVER MARKS AND STANDARDS

Since the end of the nineteenth century, silver in France has been designated by a silver mark of the head of Minerva, wearing a helmet and looking to the right. If the piece is secondhand, or acquired abroad, it is stamped with a weevil (beetle) or a swan.

Like gold, silver has several degrees of fineness (the proportion of precious metal found in an alloy). The degree reflects the quantity of copper used. In France, the finest silver is made with 925 parts silver and 75 parts copper, as reflected by the 925/1000 mark engraved on the metal. In English speaking countries, the metal often bears the engraving "pure sterling."

IT LOOKS LIKE SILVER!

Up until the end of the eighteenth century, it was common practice to weld a thin leaf of silver to a sheet of copper to obtain silver-plated metal.

Maillot and Chorier were the first in France to perfect an alloy of copper, zinc, and nickel that imitated perfectly

✳ Giving patina to silver

Javel water quickly blackens silver jewelry, giving a patina to a jewel that might have been too flashy before. Let the jewelry soak for a few seconds, long enough for it to take on a tint. Rinse and shine with a soft cloth.

the appearance of white metal. Named "Maillechort" after its inventors, the metal is plunged into a bath of silver salts, which settle on the surface by means of electrolysis.

In North Africa, alloys of copper and zinc were often used to imitate silver. It can be difficult at times to distinguish zamak from solid silver.

In Southeast Asia, nickel has long been used as an alloy; the result is often known as "alpaca silver." In Burma, Laos, and Cambodia, mountain tribes continue to make large quantities of jewelry from this alloy or from hollow silver, which is light and fragile.

SILVER AROUND THE WORLD

In Spain, solid silver is frequently cheaper than in France.

Left

When rings become large enough to be worn as bracelets they are called bangles. Mix them up and listen to them clink as you move.

Above right

Antique silver ring in marquise setting with moonstones and turquoise. Over time, the silver acquires a beautiful patina, and its edges soften. It is important to check the setting regularly as the prongs wear down and the stones may become loose.

Scandinavian jewelry, often sober and refined, is much esteemed for the high quality of its design. Jewelers there have not hesitated to choose silver for their beautiful creations, occasionally enhanced by a piece of Baltic amber or a moonstone. Georg Jensen, the well-known Danish jeweler, has made superb pieces in the style of art nouveau, and his company remains among the most important in the world of contemporary silver design.

Jewelry made by the Navajos is equally famous. Crafted from solid silver, the pieces are often decorated with turquoise. Sadly, their success has had a detrimental effect on their art: jewelry

Previous pages
Silver is a soft metal that oxidizes and blackens. Felt is an ideal material to gently protect it, especially when you have collectible pieces such as these little hearts and a ring by Peter Bauhuis.

* ## The weak link

When purchasing a chain, it is important to check the condition of the links: on the spot where they rub against each other, the metal can wear thin and break. Once they are repaired and welded back together, the links will show a visible trace from the welding.

made today is only of a mediocre quality when compared with those much admired pieces made as recently as the 1960s and 1970s, which are now collectors' items.

HOW TO BUY ANTIQUE PIECES

Silver is a soft metal that dents, scratches, and bends easily. It is important to make sure that such damage is not too evident. Rings are especially fragile. A silver band can become as thin as a sheet of paper.

Hollow silver is most likely to show scars from its earlier life. Sometimes these pieces cannot be repaired. It is impossible to repair dents on a bangle or drop earrings, no matter how thick the silver leaf.

Left
Small silver cross from the nineteenth century, decorated with rock crystal and natural pearls. Before buying a piece of jewelry like this, examine it carefully to ensure that it is not missing a pearl, the stones are not damaged, and the bail clasp is solid.

Right
To give your silver back its shine, enclose the tarnished jewelry in a pouch of aluminum foil and place it in a pot of boiling water. Wait several minutes and then let it cool. Upon opening the package, you will rediscover your shining jewels.

✳ Jewelry brush

This item is indispensable for cleaning the crevices and relief work on engraved jewelry. It is best to choose a soft-bristled brush, which slides into the smallest recesses.

CARE AND MAINTENANCE

Silver jewelry that is exposed to the air and sunlight oxidizes and tarnishes quickly. It is important to put silver away and to separate it from any other type of metal that can tarnish or scratch it.

Protect fragile pieces, particularly those made with hollow silver, by wrapping them individually in a soft cloth—either felt or silk is best for the most delicate pieces.

The best way to maintain the luster of your silver is to wear it as often as possible, but certain types of skin, because they are more acidic, can cause silver to oxidize.

Cleaning products made for silver tableware should not be used on silver jewelry unless the piece is extremely dirty. Never use one of these products on silver decorated with gemstones.

The best silver cleaner can be found at your local pharmacy and in some supermarkets: baking soda. The simplest method is to pour some of the soda powder into your damp hands and then gently rub the jewelry until its original color and shine return. To reach into the contours of embossed or carved silver, use a damp toothbrush whose bristles have been softened by previous use. You can also add a drop of liquid detergent to the baking soda. Rinse the jewelry in water and dry with a piece of fine cloth.

Toothpaste is another good choice for cleaning silver, but it is not suited for the care of antique jewelry, particularly if it is engraved or carved. The paste tends to slip into the cracks and dries quickly. If necessary, you can remove the white marks with pure alcohol.

Lemon juice shines silver and wipes away blemishes. You can simply rub the jewelry against a slice of lemon or, for rings and other carved silver items, use a soft-bristled brush dipped in lemon juice to rub the jewelry.

Left

Baking soda is the ideal cleaning product for silver (as well as gold).

✳ For the sensitive types

Certain skin types do no react well with silver (or other common metals), which can sometimes result in irritations. In this case, the only solution is to wear pure gold.

OLD-FASHIONED RECIPES

To restore the shine to severely oxidized silver, roll it in a sheet of aluminum foil and plunge into a pot of boiling salted water. The salt is optional, but it helps to activate the process. Leave the package in the pot for about ten minutes, then remove from the pot and open up the foil. The sheet of foil should have absorbed all of the oxidation and should now be black. Rinse the newly shined piece of jewelry and you are done. This method should not be used with jewelry decorated with pearls or other precious gemstones.

Left

This transparent jewelry box offers the advantage of visibility. With its multiple compartments, it is easy to arrange chains, necklaces, rings, and other items. Meticulous collectors can use each drawer to separate treasures by material or other categories.

Right

A coat of clear or antiallergenic nail polish may be applied to rings or snaps that come into contact with the skin to keep them from irritating your skin.

Gemstones

Immemorial
and Eternal

The Sparkle of Stones

Mankind has always sought a divine origin for inexplicable natural phenomena. Thus, gemstones discovered by chance in a river or shimmering in the dark depths of a gold mine have given rise to the creation of many myths and legends.

There are only four precious stones: diamonds, emeralds, rubies, and sapphires. The carat of these precious stones is purely a weight designation: 1 carat is equal to 0.2 grams.

The Diamond, an Immortal Light

«. . . it may be that some of the rain of ancient diamonds falling to the earth seeded the diamonds we mine today. In this model, the diamond on someone's finger might contain at its center a dot of a jewel whose antiquity goes back ten billion years.» Matthew Hart, *Diamond*, Plume, 2002.

Diamonds were certainly born with the universe, even before the formation of the earth and the sun. They are made of pure carbon (like coal!) crystallized in the earth's crust under the combined effects of pressure and heat.

The emblem of kings and power, this stone has always aroused the most extravagant dreams.

The word "diamond" derives from the ancient Greek word *adamas*, meaning invincible or untamed, as it was very difficult to cut and polish diamonds with the methods available in ancient times.

It is the purest and hardest of all stones. Nothing can destroy it, apart from extreme heat. The only way to scratch a diamond is with another diamond, and only diamond dust can shape or polish a diamond.

FROM INDIA TO SOUTH AFRICA

Up until the seventeenth century, the most beautiful diamonds were extracted from India. They came from the great region of Golconda, near the current town of Hyderabad. The maharajah's jewels bear witness to the abundance of stones from this valley.

Certain Indian diamonds have become legends, such as the Koh-i-Noor (Persian for "Mountain of Light"), which was extracted from the Kollur mine. In the sixteenth century, it fell into the hands of the conqueror Baber, the Mogul emperor of India; it was later

The rose cut is one of the oldest diamond cuts. The Jeannette cross from the eighteenth century, the heart, and the small bird shown here are all charming examples. The rose cut has fewer facets, so the stones are not as reflective. To enhance their brilliance, they were sometimes mounted in clinquant setting: a thin sheet of metal foil was placed under the pavilion of the diamond.

obtained by the Punjab rajahs and finally taken away by the English. In 1850, the Koh-i-Noor left its original home to adorn the crown of Queen Victoria, and it still adorns the crown of the British sovereign.

Diamonds also come from Brazil. However, at the end of the nineteenth century, a major revolution occurred in industrial diamond mining in South Africa. This country now produces the greatest number of diamonds, due largely to the work of a company that holds a quasi monopoly over the world market: De Beers.

TRANSPARENCY AND COLOR

A beautiful diamond must be perfectly pure. When examined with a loupe, which magnifies an object ten times, the most beautiful diamonds show no defects or inclusions called "flaws."

Transparent diamonds are the most common, but there are also colored diamonds: blue, green, yellow, pink, and even red, along with brown diamonds with varying degrees of light and dark. These natural colors are rare and much more precious. For this reason, there is a temptation to change the color through certain procedures such as irradiation.

Certainly one of the most famous diamonds is the Hope diamond; an intense blue stone, it is believed to have brought bad luck to its successive owners. It can be admired today without risk in a visit to the Smithsonian Institution in Washington, DC.

ANTIQUE AND MODERN CUTS

In the past, raw diamonds were simply polished and cut according to their natural form. Sometimes they were mounted in a closed setting (the metal grips the stone, and the pavilion is not visible), backed with a sheet of metal foil called a "clinquant," in order to accentuate the diamond's brilliance.

One of the oldest cuts of diamonds is the rose cut. The difference is made very clear by simply placing a diamond of this cut next to a modern diamond. There are fewer facets, giving the stone its "rose" shape, with a domed crown and a flat base.

The brilliant cut with a set of 57 facets, invented in the seventeenth century, was conceived to maximize the light reflected from the stone. It allows a myriad of shapes to be created from the raw stone: oval, cushion (square or round), heart shaped, pear (drop shaped), marquise (boat shaped), or briolette (drop shaped with multiple facets).

The emerald and baguette cuts produce rectangular shapes that are fairly narrow with a flat top called the "table." Some people appreciate the older diamond cuts or even the polished raw stones. Their natural and mysterious glimmer is unlike the sparkling modern-cut diamond.

✳ The four Cs

A diamond is valued according to the four "Cs": carat (weight), cut, clarity, and color.

Today, cutting is computerized and automated. All the data about the stone is analyzed by a computer, which allows the maximum profit and brilliance to be derived from the raw diamond, while losing only the smallest volume from the original stone.

IT LOOKS LIKE A DIAMOND!

The Englishman Ravanscroft used lead crystal for the first time in the eighteenth century, cutting it into facets to imitate diamonds. This new material, first sold in Paris by the jeweler Georges Strass, gained universal recognition under the name "strass." (In England, this crystalline material is called "paste.")

Left

Reproduction from the Encyclopedia of Diderot & d'Alembert, *showing the various diamond cuts.*

Right

In all its splendor and priceless simplicity, here is a magnificent solitaire (single-mounted stone) signed by De Beers. The facets and the perfection of the cut play with light and transparency while the reflection is lost in the heart of the stone.

✳ Sparkling diamonds

To make them shimmer, soak diamonds in alcohol and rub briskly on all sides, paying special attention to areas where dirt has accumulated—especially for rings that are worn every day.

Produced by the greatest jewelers and mounted into gold and silver with richly polished and cut settings, strass jewelry looked real, especially under gas lamps and later under electric lights. Many people were fooled. Certain women would not hesitate to pass off their strass as real diamonds. This is, of course, the theme of the short story by Guy de Maupassant entitled *The Necklace*. A young woman lends her best friend a diamond necklace. The friend loses it during a soiree, bringing ruin upon herself for the rest of her life so that she may buy a replacement. Many years later, when the two friends meet again, the truth is revealed: the stones were fake!

At the end of the nineteenth century, strass that was set with industrial methods lost its popularity.

As an imitation material, colorless zircon (or white sapphire) is now the most convincing. However, these stones never offer the sparkle of a real diamond. Also, they deteriorate and yellow over time.

Recently, some industrial diamond producers have proposed an astonishing procedure to recreate the authenticity of diamonds using the ashes from cadavers. But, in this case, it is not perfection that is at stake.

A NOTE

Diamonds do not deteriorate, but a major shock can crack them. However, this would be a rare accident.

In order for your diamonds to reflect their ultimate sparkle, they must be cleaned regularly. If not, they will tarnish and lose their initial clarity. They can be washed in soapy water with a soft-bristled toothbrush. You can also use rubbing alcohol.

Rings should be taken off before washing hands as the soap can stick to the pieces, and certain delicate jewels do not withstand contact with water well.

The Gardens
of Emerald

The emerald is the most beautiful of the
beryls. Its name derives from the Greek
word *smaragdos*, which means "the precious blue and green water from the
sea." In ancient times, it symbolized
energy and eternal beauty.

The most beautiful emeralds come
from Colombia, and their origin is
laden with legend. When the conquistadors came to Colombia, they noticed the
brilliant green stones in the gullets of
the wild turkeys they ate. Following after
the fowl, the Spaniards found the most
astounding emerald mine: the Muzo
mine. This site is still mined, producing the most beautiful stones.

The top jewelers place great value
on "old-mine emeralds," which were
extracted from Muzo over a century ago.
Madagascar also produces beautiful
emeralds. They are clearer than the
Colombian stones, but are very pure and
show few fissures.

Emeralds often have inclusions,
which look like small plants. When the
emerald is spread with inclusions that
look like a field of wild grass, the fissures
are transformed into "jardins," a condition that makes the stonecutter's work
much more difficult.

THE DEEPEST GREEN

The emerald is green—a special col-
oration that emanates from the presence
of chromium oxide. There are also
lighter and darker shades that range
from pale to blue or yellow, with the
latter being of lesser value.

THE CUT

Antique emeralds were simply polished
and cut into cabochons—a rounded and
smooth shape without any facets. The
step cut, or emerald cut, is the most
characteristic for this stone. It has four
apparent angles and a plane surface
called the "table."

IT LOOKS LIKE AN EMERALD!

Since ancient times, colored green stones
have been passed off as emeralds. They
are detectable from their surface wear
and the absence of inclusions.

Synthetic emeralds, which appeared
at the beginning of the twentieth century, are often of such good quality that
they are difficult to detect with the naked
eye. This stone is called an emerald dou-
blet: a thin strip of stone (rock crystal,
aquamarine, or pale emerald) or ordi-
nary glass is glued onto a base that is colored green to give the illusion of an
authentic emerald.

✳ Color above all

An emerald with a rich and smooth color, similar to a luscious mint candy, has
more value than a larger pale stone, even if it shows inclusions.

Rubies, Red for Passion

In the corundum family, there are two siblings that are nearly identical in appearance. While the ruby is characterized by its red color, the sapphire comes in all sorts of hues. There is even a sapphire so pink that one hesitates before placing it in one or the other category.

A stone that was extremely rare in ancient times, the ruby was reserved for emperors, kings, and princes. Its name comes from the Latin *rubeus* (meaning red), an adjective that designates all stones of this color. It is a symbol of happiness often associated with love and loyalty, and known as the stone for engagement rings par excellence. Some people believe that rubies also give strength to people who are nervous or timid.

When it is the color of pigeon blood, an especially fiery and glistening red, the ruby is the second most valuable stone after the diamond. The most beautiful rubies come from Burma, in particular from the mines of Mogok. It is said that one can walk on the rubies there!

SHADES OF RED

Mogok rubies are the color of pigeon blood; rubies from Thailand are the color of cow blood, with a spot of purplish brown; and those from Sri Lanka are described as pink with a spot of purple. Rubies fall within a wide range of reds—the shiny color explained by

Left

Unfaceted rubies from Adelline. The stone, which is very large, is cut en cabochon and polished in an old-fashioned style.

Right

A flawless, dark-colored, and silky ruby can fetch mind-boggling sums, even higher than a diamond of similar size and quality. But a beautiful spinel, which is less costly, can be just as beautiful; spinels have been often mistaken for rubies. This ruby swivel ring mounted in 22-karat gold and this chain with sequins of pure gold alternating with rubellites are creations of Marie-Hélène de Taillac.

the presence of chromium oxide. The most important aspects of the stone are the depth of color and velvety smoothness, which should be lively without being garish.

Rubies are rarely pure. They contain inclusions called "silk" that scatter light. They do not reduce the value of the stone as long as they do not alter its transparency and clarity.

When these inclusions take the shape of a star, they may actually increase the price. These are, of course, star rubies, which are cabochon cut.

IT LOOKS LIKE A RUBY!

Our forefathers were often fooled and assumed that the most beautiful red stones were rubies.

The advent of modern techniques of identification has allowed us to differentiate and specify the spinels, which were once called "balas rubies." Rubellites, which are raspberry red tourmalines, adorned the oldest royal crowns. Certain very beautiful and high-quality garnets may also have been confused with rubies.

During ancient times, even colored glass was used to imitate rubies.

Synthetic rubies reflect a color that is too clear, without depth, and they contain no inclusions.

RUBIES AROUND THE WORLD

When traveling to Thailand, Burma, or other places known for their precious stone mines, people are often tempted to buy stones, hoping for a good deal. But buyers should beware. With techniques such as heating and irradiation, the aspects of the stones can be modified, especially their color. Furthermore, an invisible crack can be disguised with an injection of resin, which is undetectable to the naked eye. Unless you are a gemologist, it is difficult to know the real value of a stone.

The Spiritual Power of the Sapphire

In the past, priests wore a sapphire on their right hand—the hand they used to bless. It was said that the blue of the sapphire was the color of the celestial vault, and that this color could calm the ardor of love. Sapphires were also considered emblems of wisdom and meditation. For Buddhists, they represent a link between the material and spiritual worlds. Sapphires are also said to encourage love and fidelity, making them the perfect stone to commemorate an engagement.

These stones most often symbolize the power associated with faith.

Right

A dragonfly brooch in typical art nouveau style. The movable wings are ornamented with rose-cut diamonds and pale sapphires, while the central sapphire is a deeper color.

✳ **While traveling in Asia: avoid impulse buys**

▪ It is advisable to avoid buying from street vendors or anyone without a reputation in the business. Also, ignore advice from local taxi drivers, who may be getting a kickback.

▪ When buying a valuable precious stone, always ask for a certificate describing the stone and specifying its weight in carats.

CELESTIAL BLUE AND OTHER HUES

When you talk about a sapphire, blue is the color that immediately comes to mind (it comes from the presence of iron oxide): cornflower blue, cerulean blue, sea blue, indigo, and royal blue. This is a wide palette, evoking the sky at all hours of the day. The darkest sapphires, which resemble the color of night or even the color of ink, have less value than a stone that is totally clear and pure, reflecting light magnificently.

The color range also extends to pinks and yellows. The lotus flower sapphire, also known as the pink orange padparadscha, is rare and highly sought after by lapidaries. Fakes abound.

A PRECIOUS STAR

Like rubies, sapphires have many inclusions that are as thin as threads of silk. When these inclusions appear as lines, they exhibit an optical quality that forms the shape of a six-pointed star; these are called star sapphires.

These stones are usually cut into cabochons, along with large stones, which have so many inclusions that they become opaque.

A NOTE

This stone is not very fragile as it is extremely hard.

Left

Adelline, a jeweler working in India, appreciates the natural beauty of large stones that are cut simply and polished, as was the case in ancient times. Yves Gratas prefers a cabochon or faceted cut, depending on the color of the stone.

Above right

An insect sitting on a leaf—what could be more natural! The leaf is made of bronze, set with tiny diamond drops, and the small fly from the 1960s is made of gold and sapphires.

The Heart of Stones

«Man wants them for their long life, their strength, their intransigence and their brilliance, their smoothness and their impenetrability, whether whole or broken. They are fire and water in the same immortal transparency, sometimes seen with the iris, sometimes in a mist. Whosoever holds them in his palm, carries with him the purity, the cold and the distance of the stars, a great serenity.» Roger Caillois, *Stones*, Éditions Gallimard, 1971.

The Enigmatic Agate

«I am talking about stones. On the edge of a dream, a ferment, an image; a stone that can appear as a wisp of hair, opaque and stiff like the head of a drowned man, which has not been driven away by the water . . . there in a blue canal where the life force becomes more visible and more vulnerable.» This text by Roger Caillois expresses the quintessence of the universe of agates. These stones have fascinated mankind since antiquity.

Their name derives from the Sicilian river, the Achates, where they were first discovered in ancient times. The cornelian, a red agate, was worn as a magic amulet and talisman to protect against sickness—hemorrhages in particular. As with coral, this superstition was linked to its red color.

Agates were engraved with initials (intaglio engraving motif) or chiseled and sculpted in relief to make cameos.

Left

These jewels date from the nineteenth century, presenting various aspects of "riband agates." The rounded brooch is Scottish and is characteristic of the Victorian period. Agates were often worn by people in mourning, who were prohibited from wearing valuable or colorful stones.

An Infinite Variety

Agates form an enigmatic labyrinth in which the collectors can easily lose themselves. There are so many types: gray, amber, brown, golden, coppery red, milky white such as chalcedony, black, and striped with distinct bands. Onyx is the black version of agate.

While they can never be used as jewelry, one of the most fascinating agates is certainly the water agate. Imagine a geode perfectly enclosed like a stone reliquary enclosing immemorial water, "the water so hidden you can only see the shadows moving, only your ears can hear the lapping," (Roger Caillois) which was deposited in the interior when the universe was formed. Alas, a slight shock or a miniscule crack might cause all of this to evaporate forever.

Eye agate beads called "Dzi" have been sought after since antiquity as magic stones, especially the sacred agates from Tibet that ward off the evil eye. These beads bear a pattern of different colored layers, ranging from brown to white. They are cut and polished into cabochons, maximizing the dark spot at the center that looks like an eye. Collectors will fight for them, paying thousands of dollars for those that are perfectly shaped and well cut.

The nicolo agate ("small eye") is a variant of the eye agate bead, with gray blue layers against a darker background.

In the eighteenth century, moss agates, also called dendritic or plantlike,

✳ Charms, amulets, and fetishes

Since ancient times, people have adorned themselves with figures that serve both as ornaments and as amulets. Most jewelers carry a collection of good luck charms. Collectors prefer to unearth them in secondhand stores and flea markets.

were highly valued, as they showed capricious patterns suggestive of vegetation, such as lichens or petrified trees, imprisoned for eternity in a mineral coating.

IT LOOKS LIKE AN AGATE!

Glass has been used to imitate agate since ancient times. There are certain old beads that are so well made that they may fool you. Their surface usually shows signs of wear, and if you knock the bead against your teeth, it does not make the same sound as a stone. Also the color seems "painted," and there will be a sort of central core (where the thread passes through) that is lighter.

Left

Dzi or magic eye. This very special agate is cut in successive layers that reveal white lines against a dark background. Collectors compete with each other for these stones, especially in Asia, where their protective virtues are highly valued. If the stone is pierced, it can be threaded with gold cord to make a ring or necklace.

Right

A heart, a four-leaf clover, and a clenched fist (known as figa in Brazil) are some of the most popular good luck charms. Made of yellow agate and quartz, these are from Brazil.

✳ The power of the skin

When jewels set with precious stones are worn against the skin, they can subtly change color, acquiring an unexpected luster.

Spinel, Thorn of Fire

Called "little thorn" because of the sharp points of its crystals, this stone was often confused with the ruby.

Spinels exhibit many inclusions and sometimes show dark spots called "macles."

A GREAT DIVERSITY OF COLOR

Spinels come in a wide range of deep reds, but they may also be pink, gray, blue, green, or colorless.

The lively red spinels used to be called "balas rubies." This name is now prohibited to avoid confusion.

CARE AND MAINTENANCE

Spinel is a relatively hard stone, but due to its inclusions, which can be numerous, it may become fragile. In India, jewelers confirm that spinel improves with delicate oil baths. The oil gives the stone a glow and can fill in certain very obvious inclusions if the bath is hot and long.

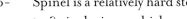

Left

Some stones, like this pink spinel, contain multiple inclusions. They can be seen clearly in this glass where the ring is soaking in a bath of fine oil. The oil seeps into the miniscule cracks and temporarily gives the stone back its clarity and luminosity.

Above right

A necklace of tourmalines arranged in a silk pouch, where the stones are protected.

Quartz and Rock Crystal

Quartz is a large family that includes many stones such as amethyst, aventurine, citrine, and rock crystal. In ancient times, it was believed that rock crystal was formed from eternal ice fossilized at the top of mountains. Its Greek name, *krysallos*, means "ice."

While rock crystal is as transparent in color as its water source, quartz can also be blue, mauve, pink, yellow, pale green (lemon quartz), smoky brown (smoky quartz), or black.

✳ Clasps and fasteners

Depending on their shape, the period when they were created, and their weight, earrings come with all types of clasps. The swan neck is the simplest and oldest style: a bent metal stem that passes through the pierced hole of the ear.

Quartz sometimes exhibits inclusions. When these appear in the shape of golden or copper hairs, the quartz is called rutilated quartz or Venus' hair stone.

AMETHYST, A HIGHLY PRIZED STONE

Amethyst is mauve or violet quartz. Its name, of Greek origin, means "the stone that preserves from drunkenness" as these ancient people believed that the violet color (like the flower of the same name) protected them from inebriation!

Its color ranges from pale mauve, almost pink, to the deepest violet. Amethyst was used by priests, as it was believed to be spiritual and protect from all drunkenness. At the beginning of the twentieth century, it was often cut into heart shapes, a talisman that was supposed to bring good luck.

Left

A ring created by Sylvie Pélissier, embellished with a double band of amethyst and garnet beads. The unpolished amethyst ring shows the different shades of this stone— from extremely pale mauve to intense violet.

Right

Faceted crystal pendant earrings made from rock crystal and silver and large shimmering drop earrings made from pale amethyst. They are shown hanging from an antique bronze holder.

SHIMMERING CITRINE

When quartz is beautiful amber, cognac, or a golden yellow color, it is called citrine. Citrine should not be confused with noble topaz (a term used by jewelers), which is amber and pinkish yellow and is much more rare and valuable.

Citrine has been used often since the beginning of the nineteenth century because of its sunlike color. This gem is reputed to enhance artistic endeavors and creativity and to generate energy.

The Garnet, Stone of Bohemia

Does its name come from the fruit of the pomegranate tree, whose translucent seeds are colored in shades of red and pink, or from the Latin word *granatus*, meaning "stones of grain"? Etymologists have not reached an agreement on this subject. Highly valued in ancient times, it embellished many royal jewels. Due to its deep red color, it was sometimes called a carbuncle.

Found often in Bohemia, where there were a large number of stonecutting workshops, garnets adorned many pieces of Austro-Hungarian jewelry that were made with gold, vermeil, or silver nielloware. The stones were cut into cabochons or facets and were sometimes combined with turquoise in a clinquant setting—using a metal foil to enliven their sparkle or simply gilded at the base.

Left

When a drop of water is placed on this real garnet, the drop remains aligned to the curve of the stone. This proves that the stone is authentic. Another way to tell the difference between garnet and glass: a stone is very cold to the touch, while glass heats up faster.

Right

Various aspects of the garnet were used for earrings in nineteenth-century France and Italy, such as these hoops made in India and this multistrand necklace of faceted stones that look like pomegranate seeds.

✳ Garnets and carbuncles

Garnets have been highly valued over many centuries for their deep red color. This color, which is as red as blood, has contributed to belief in the garnet's protective and magical attributes. It was once said that the garnet symbolized courage and energy. It is sometimes called a carbuncle stone (when it is a bright red).

RED, ORANGE, GREEN

The most common garnets are deep, dark red, bright red, or pink tinted with mauve. However, there are other varieties that are more rare and valuable, which occur in different hues.

The demantoid garnet is a deep green color. It sparkles like a diamond, and hence its name is derived from *demant*, which means "diamond" in old German. Its value can be equal to that of a diamond.

Another highly sought-after garnet is the tsavorite, which is mint green in color and categorized as a grossularite. This type of garnet is the color of green absinthe, evoking gooseberries; hence it is often called a gooseberry garnet.

Certain grossular garnets may also be orange: the mandarin-colored stones are the most highly prized by jewelers for their vivacity and luminosity.

IT LOOKS LIKE A GARNET!

Since ancient times, glass was used to imitate garnets. When viewed in the light of day, miniscule spherical bubbles appear in the glass.

To ensure that the stones are authentic, here is some advice from an old book of magic: "You must be fully undressed, wearing only your stone. Slather your body in honey and lie down near some flies or wasps. If they do not come near you, you know you have a garnet; but if the contrary occurs, it is a fake." The water drop test seems more convincing!

Synthetic stones and artificially colored glass are used to imitate the tsavorite and the demantoid garnets, which are currently in great demand.

Left

This beautiful red cabochon looks like a garnet, but if you look at it closely, you will see round bubbles on the inside. It contains a slight crack, foliated through several layers. And when water is dropped on its surface, the liquid spreads out immediately. Other tests indicate that it is colored glass.

✳ Jade is not always green

Jade exists in an infinite range of colors, from black to mauve, and from yellow to pink. It is a stone that has been often imitated with glass, resin, Bakelite, and various other materials. Imperial jade, which is an emerald green color—quite rare and very expensive—is one of the most commonly imitated jades.

The World of Jade

In ancient China, people would ruin themselves for rare and precious stones. Jade was one of those stones. The emblem of perfection, it symbolized the five essential Chinese virtues: charity, modesty, courage, justice, and wisdom. The incarnation of yang (strength), jade was also the stone in which the Pi symbol was cut—a flat disk with a hole in the center through which the emperor would look at the world. It was also the stone of the imperial seal.

Its name is affiliated with superstition: this green stone, the color of bile, was believed to heal ailments of the liver. In Spanish, it was called *pieta de hijada* (stone of the liver), from which the English word "jade" was derived. According to lapidaries, there are two types of jade: Burmese jadeite and Chinese nephrite (literally meaning the "kidney stone"). Jadeite is greener than nephrite and is sometimes tinted with tones of brown and yellow.

THE GREEN IS WHAT COUNTS

There is a variety of jadeite that is extremely precious and sought after as much as imperial jade. This stone is literally the color of emerald green and was reserved in the past solely for the emperor of China.

Jadeite appears in a large range of opaque and translucent colors: luminous green jade and white with varying degrees of green, pink, mauve, gray, reddish brown, and gray blue. Nephrite tends to be yellow-tinted green, bright green, dark green, grayish or creamy white, or brown yellow.

IT LOOKS LIKE JADE!

Some stones have a similar appearance to jade. This is the case with serpentine—a green, veined marble—as well as chalcedony, which is milky white or green.

Glass is often used to imitate jade, but has spherical bubbles that are easily recognizable.

A long sautoir made of jade beads, in the popular style favored during the 1920s.

A jumble of green necklaces in which the authentic jade necklace is hidden (second from top). The necklace with an eggplant pendant is made of translucent serpentine. The others are paste necklaces made of glass.

✳ **Attention! Fragile !**

If you own a jade bracelet, wear it on the wrist of the arm you use less. You will thus avoid banging or breaking it when you go about your daily routine.

CARE AND MAINTENANCE

As it is a porous stone, jade is relatively fragile. It does not react well to alcohol or lotions: do not spray perfume or apply lotion on your neck before putting on a jade necklace.

Be careful not to hit your jade against a hard material, as it will crack and break easily. Some superstitious people believe that if jade cracks or breaks, it portends an accident or bad luck.

Lapis Lazuli, a Gift from the Sky

Literally called "the stone of the sky" by the Greeks, it was considered by the Sumerians to be a gift from the heavens. The Egyptians, who prized it highly, brought it from Afghanistan, using it to adorn many of their necklaces, bracelets, and scarab amulets so that such jewelry has been found in abundance.

The color of indigo blue—"the color of the nocturnal sky shimmering with gold"—it is dusted with miniscule flecks of pyrite, a metallic oxide that shines like nuggets of gold or silver.

In Europe, ground-up lapis lazuli was used as a rare and precious pigment in the past, which painters called ultramarine blue because it came from Afghanistan—a land on the other side of the Mediterranean. It is this blue color that gave the almost unreal luminosity to the primitive paintings of Italian artists, such as Fra Angelico and Piero della Francesca.

THE BLUE OF THE SKY

Lapis lazuli owes its luminous blue color to the presence of lazurite. The stone is considered to be of the highest quality when the blue is homogenous, without apparent and multiple yellowish or white veins caused by a large quantity of calcite.

However, be careful if the stone is too uniform and without a mark. The stones are often bathed in dye to enhance their brilliance, and stones such as chalcedony and white agate are sometimes dyed to appear as lapis.

Right

Two lapis necklaces of perfect quality, lustrous and with stones of a deep color. The pendant is adorned with miniscule diamonds, representative of the art deco style. The blue color of the lapis reflects a constellation of brilliant flecks that reveal the iron pyrite content.

Left

The reflections created by opals borrow their colors from the rainbow. Sometimes blue dominates, then a red flame lights under a pale light. Mined in Mexico, fire opal is recognizable from its surprising orange color.

The Magical Opal

Almost like a piece of the rainbow that has fallen onto earth, all the colors of the opal are concentrated in its core. The opal has been the subject of many superstitions, especially during the nineteenth century. The Russians believed it gave off the evil eye. In England, a novel by Walter Scott entitled *Anne of Geierstein* spread the idea that the opal brought bad luck. In France, some people still mistrust this stone today. In Asia, to the contrary, it is the symbol of hope and is believed to be placed under the protection of the gods.

Its bad reputation must certainly derive from its extreme fragility, dreaded by those who had to work with it. It is a soft and porous stone, composed of mineralized silica gel and a small quantity of water (6 to 10 percent).

The majority of opals come from Australia, but they can also be found in Brazil (of a lower quality) and in Mexico.

FROM WHITE TO BLACK

The milky white opalescent opal is quite common, but there are other colors: the fire opal from Mexico is an incandescent red, the black opal is tinted dark blue with red streaks, and there are also pale pink opals, as well as amber yellow.

IT LOOKS LIKE AN OPAL!

In the nineteenth century, glassmakers invented a milky white glass called opaline, which they used to make jewelry. However, it looks obviously like glass.

There is also a variety of iridescent agate that evokes the shimmering of butterfly wings.

CARE AND MAINTENANCE

A porous and fragile stone, the opal may split, break, or change color. When you wear an opal ring, be careful not to hit it against hard surfaces. Be sure to take it off before washing your hands as the soap may penetrate the interior of the stone and change its iridescence.

✳ Your opal may be thirsty!

This stone has a strange characteristic: it holds water. When the opal becomes dehydrated in an inert, dry, and hot atmosphere, it loses its reflection and also seems to lose strength. Sometimes jewelers hide a small glass of water in the corner of their store windows. This is to maintain humidity in the air. At home you can soak your opals in water to hydrate them.

Wash opals with clear water and wipe with a soft cloth; a piece of silk is ideal.

It is not recommended that you store an opal necklace or bracelet in a cloth in a closed box: the cotton absorbs the natural humidity and can bring about a slow end to the stones.

Heat is harmful, as is extreme cold.

Last piece of advice: do not spray perfume or apply moisturizer before wearing an opal piece. The oil from the lotion will clog the pores of the opal, which breathes like skin. If it loses its luster, you can take it to a jeweler to have it repolished.

The Tourmaline, In Every Color

The tourmaline is currently in high demand around the world. It is one of the stones that jewelers prefer for its rich array of color, transparency, and sparkle.

A Rainbow

Certain tourmalines are polychromatic. There is even a variety that is pink and green, evoking a slice of watermelon.

Tourmaline has an expansive color range: from colorless to black, passing through raspberry red (rubellite), green, blue (indicolite), gray, and brown.

There are also glistening amber-colored stones called cat's-eye.

The Cut

Tourmaline is usually faceted. When it has a large number of inclusions that make it opaque, a round, oval (for necklaces), or cabochon cut is preferable.

Care and Maintenance

It is advisable to wipe these jewels regularly with a cloth moistened with oil.

✳ ## The art of the lapidary

Beautiful stones, destined for a jeweler, that are cut by hand will emit an incomparable luster. On the other hand, machine-cut stones progressively lose their luster and must be polished again.

Right

Emitting an intense luster, these hoops are made with tourmalines that were cut by hand in a workshop in Jaipur, India. They are displayed next to small machine-cut drops that appear a bit dull.

✳ Beware of imitations

Through a loupe, authentic turquoise presents microscopic white and fluffy inclusions. They can also be seen on the back side of a cabochon and on the edges of a hole made for threading. On older stones that are set in a ring, the color on the bottom is darker than the exposed color, which will have faded a bit and appear yellowish.

Celestial Turquoise

During the Middle Ages, turquoise from Persia was routed through Turkey before arriving in the West. This is what gave turquoise its name: "stones of the Turks." There was also an intense blue color used as a pigment in paintings called turquin blue, which was prepared by grinding this stone.

Along with coral and lapis lazuli, turquoise was one of the favorite stones of the Egyptians. It was included in most of their gem-decorated jewels. The Aztecs and Toltecs of Mexico also encrusted their jewels and their funerary masks with turquoise. There is a mask entirely inlaid in turquoise with shells and obsidian for the eyes, which has entranced generations of passionate Native American art fans. It is said that the most beautiful stones come from

Iran: these are Persian turquoise. They are an incomparable blue without defect—the color of the summer sky—but the continuous political turmoil in this country has made them extremely rare. Turquoise is also found in Egypt, Mexico, Australia, and California.

Turquoise was always believed to have propitious qualities. It is said to embody wisdom, along with courage, hope, and the spirit of youth. In France, in the past, it was a stone given to young girls. Like a cool stone removed from the rainbow in the sky, turquoise was often associated with the fire of garnets and the warm red of coral.

Left and above

There are many types of turquoise stones that differ in color. Turquoise from the United States is greener than turquoise from Iran, which is more sought after by jewelers for its porcelain blue hue. The necklace shown in this dish is made of unpolished American turquoise. The antique cross dates from the nineteenth century.

Right

Observed from close range, these two rings show how sensitive and fragile the turquoise material is. The color of the round cabochon ring has taken on a slight green hue over time. In addition, a crack runs across its surface due to a shock or perhaps from having been dropped. To the right, the silver ring is set with a matrix turquoise, of American origin, striped with dark lines.

✳ Sensitive stones

Avoid any contact between turquoise and oily substances such as suntan oil (be careful when wearing turquoise on a tropical vacation) and body lotions. The oil will change the original color of the stone and can make it fade; the same can happen with pearls or opals. Any contact can turn the stone greenish.

A Series of Blues

There is an interesting range of turquoise blues: the greenish blue veined with black of Tibetan turquoise, the cerulean blue of Iranian turquoise, and the intense blue of American turquoise.

Matrix turquoise is a special variety, run through with streaks of dark veins. Although spurned by gemologists, it has found favor with collectors, who see beautiful landscapes within the mysterious patterns.

It Looks Like Turquoise!

Like coral, this stone has been imitated since antiquity: the Egyptians used glass and enameled faience, bone or colored ivory, and ceramics and solidified paste that were dyed blue.

The most difficult imitations to detect are ones composed of pieces of real turquoise glued together with resin. The fact that the color is too intense, too harsh, and too uniform may help amateurs detect imitations.

If resin or some other artificial material has been used, a heated needle inserted into a fake stone will create a burning odor and a blackish hole.

Certain turquoise stones from California are injected with synthetic resin to harden them.

Today, to prevent their color from changing, turquoise is encased in a protective coating that does not hurt the quality of the stone.

Care and Maintenance

Extremely porous and fairly soft, this stone is somewhat fragile and may not endure careless handling. It does not do well in a dry atmosphere, which causes it to lose its natural humidity.

Soapy water, dust, any other liquids containing alcohol, and perfumes (alcohol and oil) are harmful.

Precious Materials

Ivory and amber do not belong to the world of stones, as they are organic materials. But, in the world of jewels, they are still considered precious materials on the same level as coral or mother-of-pearl and are popular with goldsmiths.

Ivory, the Pure Color of Africa

Ivory is an organic material that is usually crafted from elephant tusks. Fossilized Siberian mammoth tusks are also used, as are the teeth or horns of rhinoceros, hippopotamuses, sperm whales, walrus, and narwhals. The twisted horn of the narwhal (which can reach seven to ten feet in length) has a long history of legend associated with it and has appeared in numerous curiosity cabinets. During the Middle Ages, it was believed to be the horn of the unicorn.

Ivory was highly valued in Europe in the nineteenth and the beginning of the twentieth century. In France, in the town of Dieppe, sailors who spent the winter on land created a specialty, sculpting ivory to look like fine lace. This craft was also common in Asia where artisans crafted masterpieces, such as infinity rings and moving balls that are fitted one inside the other and sculpted directly on the surface of the tusk.

MARK THE DIFFERENCE

Bone, sometimes used instead of ivory, has inconsistent and intermittent streaks. Other imitations made from plastic are also veined. Patterns in the imitations are straight and more regular.

Ivory is heavy and dense to the touch. Imitations are lighter.

COLOR AND PATINA

At first, ivory is white with creamy or blond tones. Over time, it gains a patina and takes on the color of pale tea.

In the past, ivory was colored with natural products, such as saffron, verdigris, wood of Campeche trees, and oak apple (a plant parasite). Green, pink, crimson, golden yellow, or black created varying clarity for the reliefs, especially when the ivory was sculpted.

Even more surprising, during the Chinese Imperial period—where patinated ivory was prized—young mothers

Various types of jewelry made from ivory. Some are European, such as the bracelet studded with gold and the necklace adorned with beads and a heart: a work carved in Dieppe, France, in the nineteenth century. The other bracelets come from India and Africa. They have various shades of patina and color.

Right

*A bath in black tea will give
an amber tint to naturally
white ivory. It is best to choose
pieces that have a uniform
surface. Otherwise the color
will accumulate in areas that
are more heavily worn and
appear darker.*

who nursed their babies were asked to carry ivory against their breasts, as the lactic acid gives it a special tint!

On the other hand, it is more difficult to whiten ivory once it has become yellow. Some old-fashioned recipes suggest soaking it in untreated milk or buttermilk. Others advise rubbing it with a lemon wedge or with a cloth soaked in hydrogen peroxide. None of these methods is advised for older, more beautiful pieces.

Ivory should never be dried under the sun.

It Looks Like Ivory!

Some jewelry is made from dyed bone. At the end of the nineteenth century, jewelry was made from *ivoirine*, a material composed of the powder from ivory debris that was finely ground and mixed. Jewelry, including necklaces, bracelets, and earrings, made from Bakelite (synthetic resin), which may be carved, are very interesting but are not made from ivory. Created during the 1920s and 1930s and sometimes enhanced with silver or colored Bakelite, they were in style during the art deco period and eventually became collectors' items.

Since 1989, international trade in elephant ivory has been forbidden. A number of natural imitations have been created to help save the lives of the elephants in Africa.

Some of these imitations are called "vegetable ivory." This is made from corozo, the inner seed of the South American ivory palm tree, which can be worked and sculpted like ivory, taking on its color and look. While vegetable ivory may yellow, it retains a matte finish and is very porous. However, it may never be polished like ivory since it does not have the same dense grain.

✳ Life lines

Real ivory can be distinguished by its fine, sinuous, and parallel streaks that appear on the surface.

IVORY AROUND THE WORLD

Some customs officials are inflexible. They will seize any object made from ivory and will assess heavy fines on the owner. This applies especially in the United States and in India.

CARE AND MAINTENANCE

Like all organic materials, ivory is fragile.

It is particularly sensitive to changes in temperature and humidity in the air. Movements from hot to cold, along with dry air, can result in splits or at least may cause cracking.

It is thus not advisable to place the jewelry on a mantle—where the coolness of the marble may affect it—nor near a radiator—where the heat may also present a risk factor.

Cracks sometimes appear over time, leaving a fine, dark crackling appearance on the surface of the object. Splits in the material are irreparable, particularly since artisans specializing in ivory work are becoming rare.

Amber, Tear of Resin from Another Age

Amber is an organic material, but it is not at all animal in origin; it comes from the fossilized resin of conifers (*pinus succinifera*), which appeared on the earth millions of years ago. Fossilized amber should not be confused with the odorous substance by the same name used by perfumers, which is extracted from the solidified secretions of the sperm whale and gathered along the shoreline. According to Greek myth, amber was

✳ **Do not travel with your ivory**

When traveling abroad, it is preferable to leave all your ivory jewelry at home. Otherwise, you will need to take certificates of authenticity proving that you are carrying antique pieces.

born from the tears of the daughters of the sun. In a Christian legend, amber was said to have come from the tears of trees that were condemned to disappear after the flood.

In ancient times, the Greeks called amber *elektron*, because it could produce an electric charge. When it is rubbed against a piece of cloth, for example, it produces a charge of negative electricity that attracts light objects, such as a piece of paper. A conductor of current, amber has been the subject of all sorts of superstition, even more than coral or cornelian. Many rosary beads and amulets were supposed to get rid of the wearer's discontentment and bad thoughts. They were also said to predict bad luck by changing color.

In Muslim countries, where amber is often used to make both jewelry and remedies, amber has preventative qualities and is believed to offer protection from the evil eye.

A long time ago, babies were given amber bead necklaces to wear. It was thought that they would prevent irritations and reduce redness in the folds of the neck, ease teething pains, and protect from convulsions as well as sore throats.

A Fascinating Material

Amber can be transparent, translucent, or even opaque. It comes in various shades of yellow: pale yellow, blond honey, golden, orange yellow, brownish red, or even dark red. In China, slightly cloudy, green amber is valued.

Pieces of amber encapsulating fragments of animals have given rise to fanciful imaginings. Dreamers enamored with the advancement of science have been hopeful that they could revive certain species from DNA contained inside.

Opaque amber has often been cut into rounds, while translucent amber is more often faceted to reflect the light. The most beautiful faceted jewels date from the Second Empire and the beginning of the twentieth century.

It Looks Like Amber!

This natural resin has been copied since long ago with the resin from copal (tropical trees) or with colored plastic. In the 1930s, Bakelite was used.

Professionals authenticate amber with a heated needle. If the material is copal or plastic, the needle will create a black hole, and a smell of burning will be emitted. If it is made from copal, ether will also create a change in the material; upon contact, the resin will appear to gel.

As with coral, the price should be an indication. In North Africa, for example, beware of cheaper jewels sold as amber.

Care and Maintenance

Amber is a fairly fragile material, which breaks and loses its glow when it falls on a hard surface. You can try to touch up the broken parts by sanding them lightly.

Amber does not do well in a dry atmosphere and should be worn often to maintain its luster. It should be rubbed with a cloth dipped in light almond or olive oil, and then polished with a dry cloth. This is a good recipe for jewelry that appears to be covered in milky spots.

Above right

The flame test. When an object has been fabricated from a synthetic material, it does not stand up well to a heated needle: the material will melt, and the needle will make a hole. It is best to conduct this operation inside a bead or inside of a bracelet, where the results are less visible, as the needle will leave an unsightly mark on the natural ivory and amber.

Treasures
from
the Sea

Neptune's Gifts

Pearls, Daughters of the Sea

« In periods of prosperity, Hebrew women of exalted rank wore necklaces fashioned from multiple strands of pearls. The cords on which they were strung were woven from linen or wool—sometimes colored, as the Talmud reveals—and their lengths varied, so that some hung around the neck, others draped over the breast, and some even fell to the waist. » Thomas de Quincey, *Hebrew Women's Costume*, Éditions Gallimard, 1992.

Previous pages
Simple pebbles collected on the beach can be turned into jewelry, which highlights their natural beauty.

Left
From time to time, sautoirs come back into style. Freshwater pearls (Gem's Secret) and an "Alhambra" mother-of-pearl sautoir from Van Cleef & Arpels are items that remain highly successful over time.

A Short History

Pearls have been objects of envy and desire since ancient times, and their natural beauty has always evoked wonder. Their origin recalls the birth of the goddess Aphrodite who sprang to life from the sea, first appearing to mortals on the foam of a wave.

Jewelers of old used pearls from India, the island of Taprobane (now called Sri Lanka), the Red Sea, and the Persian Gulf. Natural pearls were traded throughout Asia and Europe in exchange for precious wares. The Roman emperor Caligula was famed for his pearl-encrusted boots; when he invited guests to a banquet, they gathered to feast on delicacies sprinkled with powdered gold, while sipping a concoction brewed from pearls dissolved in vinegar.

Another legendary pearl was lost forever in a chalice of vinegar—it belonged to Cleopatra. The Egyptian queen owned a pair of pendant earrings famed for their size and beauty. Determined to awe Mark Anthony with her wealth, she tossed one of them into a goblet of vinegar. After the conquest of Egypt, the second pearl was carried off to Rome where it was used to adorn the statue of Venus that stood in the Pantheon.

The scientific name for pearls is *Meleagrina margaritifera*, derived from the Greek *margaritas* (meaning "perfect beauty"). These daughters of the sea are indeed precious, but they have become increasingly scarce and are now both rare and costly. Most are cultured in the sea or freshwater.

NATURAL PEARLS AND CULTURED PEARLS

Various warm water mollusks produce pearls naturally. A small foreign object, such as a grain of sand, gets into the crustacean and creates an irritation, causing an overproduction of nacre (from the Persian *nakkar* meaning "shimmering ornament") that gradually surrounds the particle and slowly forms a pearl.

Nacre is a unique blend of calcium carbonate crystals and organic material that is deposited in layers. This particular composition produces extraordinary optical effects and gives pearls their iridescent luster and rainbow tint.

At the beginning of the twentieth century, there was a discovery that revolutionized jewelry and eventually led to the near disappearance of natural pearls. In 1920, Kokichi Mikimoto, a Japanese inventor, had the clever idea of introducing a particle of nacre and a small bit of tissue into the oysters cultivated in sea farms. Within a few years, the natural pearl trade was in ruins, as buyers showed a marked preference for the flawless, and less expensive, cultured pearls.

After the foreign particle is introduced, it takes two or three years for a pearl to form and at least five years for a high-quality gem with a thick coating of nacre. Oysters are not the only type of mollusks that produce this substance. Other gastropods, such as freshwater mussels, can also make pearls. China exports a large quantity, most of which are cultured in lakes. The most common are Biwa pearls, which sometimes have an elongated shape and are pastel or dark in color (they can be darkened by soaking them in dye). They are generally less expensive than the meleagrine and are used to make bracelets and necklaces that are affordable for all.

QUALITIES OF A FINE PEARL

A pearl's diameter may range from 8 millimeters to around 20 millimeters for the largest specimens.

Round forms are the most sought after, but other more irregular "Baroque" shapes have their own appeal and are generally less expensive than perfect spheres. Color has little effect on price, since tastes vary from one country to another. The gray pearls of Polynesia and amber-hued pearls of Australia have been highly prized over the last ten years. The American market has long preferred pearls with a pale or rose hue.

Right

Born from the sea. Baroque pearls and golden beads threaded on a cord in a style that evokes an ethnic necklace and stones chosen for their oval shape. Stones are very difficult to pierce. Unless you have a strong drill, it is advisable to seek the assistance of a jeweler.

Whatever a pearl's color or size, its luster is of the utmost importance. Jewelers seek pearls with a smooth surface that flawlessly reflects light. A pearl may be large and perfectly round, but if it has little luster, it will be less valuable than a smaller pearl with a silky, glowing radiance. However, any imperfections in the nacre will diminish its value.

FROM THE LIGHTEST TO THE DARKEST

Pearls come in many shades, from gleaming white to black and include

✳ Valuable grains

The price of a pearl depends on its size, shape, color, and luster. Stones are measured in carats, while pearls are measured in grains. Look for pearls that show no imperfections and have a fine orient.

pink, solid gray, blue gray, green (a splendid peacock hue), and gold. Darker colors are typical for pearls from Tahiti as well as some from Australia, which also produces astonishing pearls that look as if they have been dipped in gold.

Pearls are sometimes dyed and these have a uniform, consistent color. They are, of course, less expensive than natural pearls.

THEY LOOK LIKE PEARLS!

Pearls have often been imitated, especially when the only ones available were very rare and costly natural pearls.

Beginning in the eighteenth century, the French developed a process of applying a blend of animal glue and fish scales known as *essence d'orient* to a round, glass

Left

To make your own necklace with beads that have extremely miniscule holes, there are very thin needles made expressly for this purpose. You can also guide doubled-over nylon thread through the beads.

Right

Colored freshwater pearls. The dark luster of real Tahitian pearls attracts counterfeiters. Sometimes the pearls are bathed in a coloring agent that gives them all sorts of tints.

bead, giving the illusion of a genuine jewel. These were called *perles d'ablette* after the silver, scaled fish used in their production. The technique has since been refined, and today there are very good imitations, sometimes enhanced with gold or gemstones.

Keep an eye out for these in your grandmother's jewel box, a flea market, or a garage sale; you may find some wonderful surprises.

CARE AND MAINTENANCE

Fine pearls have an inimitable luster, known to connoisseurs as "orient." Pearls are living jewels and change with skin contact over time. They are naturally porous and therefore fragile.

It is often said that the more pearls are worn, the more lustrous they become. This claim may be true, if the skin in question suits the pearls, but there are cases where they mysteriously "die" and lose their natural glow. This occurs when there is excess acidity in the skin's surface, which gradually eats away at the nacre and diminishes its distinctive gleam. This problem may occur if a necklace is worn day after day or if pearls in rings or earrings are touched too

Left

Water is the pearl's natural element. To rehydrate your pearls, simply place them in a glass of slightly salted water overnight. You can also wear them into the sea. Be careful that the thread is secure (especially if it is made of silk), as it may break with frequent bathing.

✳ **A clever trick**

There is a simple method for identifying an authentic pearl immediately: rub the pearl lightly against your tooth. A fake pearl will feel as smooth as glass!

often. There is just one solution to this problem: pearls must be regularly wiped with a dampened soft cloth or rinsed in freshwater.

Pearls will also deteriorate if they are left for a long time in a closed box on a bed of cotton or some other dry material. Cotton absorbs their natural humidity and luster, resulting in fading and color change toward gray or pale tan. If this should happen, there is no remedy.

Of course, you can substitute a dip in the ocean with a glass of salt water.

Necklaces must be restrung on a regular basis, particularly when they are worn daily.

Over time, the cord will become soiled and worn and may break. If it is a valuable piece, have it restrung by a jeweler—who should use silk cord, which is both flexible and sturdy.

A knot is always tied between each pearl to prevent them from being damaged by rubbing against each other or scattering if the necklace should accidentally break.

Ill-fated alliances

Never spray perfume or place polish directly on pearls as this will damage the nacre. Be careful with any rings set with pearls when cooking; vinegar and lemon juice are fateful. Unless you want to imitate Cleopatra or Caligula . . .

CLEANING

Pearls can be easily cleaned with a damp soft cloth.

In hot countries where people may perspire heavily, pearls should be rinsed in freshwater to remove any traces of salt. Necklaces, for example, often have traces of salt at the nape of the neck and the shoulders, where pearls are in closest contact with the skin.

To revive their luster, rub pearls gently with a very soft cloth sprinkled with a few drops of sweet almond oil. They can also be rubbed between the hands.

Chemicals, such as detergents, dishwashing liquid, and strong soaps, are not recommended. Toothbrushes with hard bristles can scar the fragile surface of pearls.

Never use a jewelry cleaning product or cloth, unless it is specifically intended for cleaning pearls. Ultrasound machine cleaning can crack pearls and should never be used.

STORAGE

Pearls are fragile and should be stored separately, preferably wrapped in silk or in a soft leather case. Contact with metal or gemstone jewelry may scratch or damage pearls.

Never drop pearls on a stone floor or other hard surface because they may crack or break.

Left

When a piece of jewelry appeals to you, it is not important whether it is real or fake. These two chic costume jewelry necklaces offer proof.

Right

To maintain the luster of pearls, they must be worn often and close to the skin. Wipe them regularly with a thin and soft cloth: a silk scarf would be ideal. However, be sure to avoid spraying perfume on them.

Coral, the Tree of the Ocean

Coral is animal, vegetable, and mineral all in one. Like magical trees, its crimson branches intertwine in the darkness of the ocean's depths. It is composed of calcium carbonate secretions from animals known as polyps, which grow in colonies and connect each other by their branches, gradually creating reefs.

A Natural Curiosity

Coral is found primarily in the Mediterranean, particularly off the North African coast, around Corsica and in the Gulf of Naples. Sadly, deep sea pollution and overharvesting—sometimes outright pillaging—have steadily exhausted the supply of the Mediterranean's "red gold" resources. The warm waters off China's coast also produce coral, although it is paler in color than the most prized Mediterranean variety.

Since ancient times, people have attributed protective magical powers to jewelry crafted from blood red coral, the color of life itself. Pink and white coral are much less sought after because of their pale hues.

Superstitions Associated with Coral

The ancients believed that coral provided protection against misfortunes, tempests, and poisons.

Over the centuries, all manner of superstitions have been associated with coral. It was believed that coral would change color in the presence of a person near death or when some disaster was about to strike. Some believed that coral had the power to stop hemorrhaging and cure epilepsy.

From birth, children in Corsica and Italy wore a necklace of coral beads or a coral-branch pendant, sometimes set in gold—a tradition that continues to this day in some regions. Through generations, it was believed that the jewel protected against the evil eye and assured easier teething for nursing children. Similar beliefs are attached to amber in northern European countries.

Some Renaissance Italian paintings show the Christ child with coral jewelry, sometimes a necklace of beads or an amulet bracelet. There is also a portrait by Titian depicting Alessandro Farnese as a young man wearing a short, gold-inlaid, damascened suit of armor. The neck, cuffs, and skirt are trimmed with branches of coral, stitched on the velvet lining of the metal as protective talismans.

For centuries, amulets carved from red coral have been sold in Naples. They are either horn-shaped like little peppers or sometimes carved like a hand with the thumb folded back between the index and middle finger or with the index and ring fingers crossed to form a horn shape. Such jewelry is considered to be both ornament and good-luck charm (*jettatura* in Italian, which literally means "caster of fate").

These popular talismans can be found throughout Europe.

COLORS AND STRIATIONS

Authentic coral can by recognized by its distinctive microscopic parallel striations. A jeweler's loupe is often required to distinguish these special patterns, especially when the coral is dark in color. Coral is opaque and is not particularly heavy or light in weight. It gives off a lively sound if knocked against the teeth.

Noble coral shades range from ox-blood red, pale pink (poetically known as "angel skin coral") to white with the faintest hint of rose.

So-called white, blue, and black corals are actually madrepores and are indeed related to coral. They are not considered by jewelers to belong to the prized noble coral family, but their branches are sometimes fashioned into necklaces or used in other whimsical costume jewelry.

IT LOOKS LIKE CORAL!

The Egyptians used red glass to imitate coral, and this practice continues today. When lit from behind, glass beads are translucent. Glass also has a smooth shiny quality with no visible striations.

Bone, horn, corozo nuts, Bakelite, and dyed red plastic have all been used to make counterfeits. Today, the unsophisticated buyer's enemies are blends of powdered coral mixed with resin, a substance that can be made in any color and is very easy to shape. Forgers go so far as to etch the surface to imitate the striations of genuine coral.

☀ Well-advised purchases

To avoid being cheated, take note of the price of the jewel. A large necklace or one that has several strands of beads should be expensive if it is authentic (when sold by weight alone, coral is more expensive than gold!).

✳ Mediterranean red

Dark red coral from the Mediterranean is the most valuable. A blood red coral cabochon, the color of a ripe pepper and as big as a thumbnail, can easily fetch several hundred dollars if it is in perfect condition.

Pieces of white coral, carved and dyed red, are sometimes sold as noble coral. If these dyed materials are soaked in alcohol, the color will bleed. The artificially created red coloring is quite easy to recognize because it is often rather harsh and excessively bright, lacking the subtle shading of real coral. However, it does lend itself to fashioning impressively large necklaces.

Anything rare is costly. Red coral is scarce and therefore expensive; so expensive that necklaces crafted from branches of red or pink coral, once sold for a few dollars in souvenir shops, have become very valuable.

CORAL AROUND THE WORLD

Chinese coral is primarily used today since Mediterranean coral has largely disappeared. It can be recognized by its lighter, orangey colors.

When the black coral of southern seas is polished, it resembles lacquer and is often crafted into bangle bracelets.

Above right
Olive oil mixes well with coral and can give it a polished and shiny look if it becomes tarnished. A little trick: rub the beads against the side of your nose for an instantaneous shine!

CARE AND MAINTENANCE

Coral is an organic, porous, and fragile material. Never drop it on a hard surface because it is as breakable as glass.

If coral is soiled and darkened, a bath in olive oil is the answer. Let it soak overnight, then wipe with a paper towel. There are other remedies. You can soak it in water with a pinch of baking soda, or, as with pearls, give it a saltwater bath. Soaking necklaces repeatedly can weaken the cord; one alternative is to dip a paper towel in oil and carefully wipe the beads.

Mother-of-Pearl and Shells

Mother-of-pearl and shells have always been used to ornament the body and create jewelry. Since ancient times, various shells have been used to craft cameos, which are engraved in the thickest part of the shell. Considered less valuable than cameos crafted from agate, these works are referred to as shell cameos.

Nacre, Mother of All Pearls

The term "mother-of-pearl" is a poetic way of referring to this nacreous secretion of a mollusk. It is composed of the same material as the pearls it produces: nacre and conchioline, a type of organic substance.

Art nouveau jewelry made abundant use of the lustrous nacre with its iridescent hues, which range from light to dark.

VARYING COLORS FROM VARYING MOLLUSK

Depending on the mollusk producing the nacre, colors range from white and storm gray to steel blue, which comes from pearl-producing oysters. Freshwater mollusks produce a milky-white nacre (used for buttons, for example).

More opaque, white nacre from the Indian Ocean and rosy-white Caribbean conch (*Strombus gigas*) nacre are used to make shell cameos.

Shells, the First Jewelry

The most ancient articles of jewelry fashioned were shells that were pierced and hung from a cord. Such ornaments have been found in Paleolithic tombs dated to 28,000 BC. A collar of fossilized shells mounted with long beads and pendants was excavated in Moravia in the Czech Republic. This prehistoric piece of jewelry is evidence of the timeless urge to convert shells found on the shore into necklaces and bracelets.

Left

The gray nacre from abalones is often used to make jewelry. This medallion—decorated with an Asian-influenced photo—and the cross are contemporary designs, while the cuff links— featuring people dressed in swimsuits—date from the beginning of the twentieth century.

In Polynesia, a gift of fresh flower garlands and long shell necklaces often welcomes new visitors.

Shells were also sometimes used for less peaceful ends. The Dayak tribe in Borneo used the heart of the giant shellfish *Tridacna gigas* to craft bracelets that served both as ornaments and weapons. Worn on the right arm only by the men of the tribe, these heavy, viciously sharp bracelets could deal fatal blows to an enemy.

In Africa, the heaviest shells were shaped into rectangles with rounded corners, then pierced and strung into long necklaces and often worn in multiple strands.

A DIFFERENT KIND OF SHELL

Cowrie shells are a special case. These pretty shellfish seem to encompass all manner of primordial memories in the hollows of their shells, whose shape suggests the form of female sexual organs. Through the ages, they have served as talismans and symbols of fertility and wealth and have been used as currency or as material for ornaments and necklaces. They can be found in Tibet, Mali, Kenya, and Malaysia.

CARE AND MAINTENANCE

You can clean shells with soap and water. They can also be washed in a mixture of liquid soap and baking soda.

Left

*Antique bracelets from Indonesia and Malaysia. Cut from the shell of a polished giant clam (*Tridacna gigas*), they were worn exclusively by men from Nias Island and the Dayak tribes of Borneo. They were sometimes used as weapons.*

Right

Mexican necklace adorned with a multitude of amulets: crosses, hearts, Holy Spirit pendants, both religious and magical, called Milagros ("miracles"). These medallions have the same function as ex-votos that are hung in churches and chapels. They protect the owner.

Following page, left

A ceramic necklace by Fanny Acquart-Gensollen, made of material that looks like shells bleached over many years by the sea and the sand.

Following page, right

Keepsake shells. This small necklace was threaded and worn by a child, who then passed it on to her daughter. Many years later, by chance, they came across a matching necklace in a secondhand store.

Art and Materials

Praise for Imagination

Collectors' Materials

All sorts of creative materials have been used to fashion jewelry: ranging from grass to paper, from leather to fabric, encompassing glass, wood, horn, and even human hair and the skins of animals (elephant hair has been used to make jewelry in Africa and India).

Jewelry from Hair

Jewelry made from hair was once very popular in memorial lockets. It was considered stylish to cut off a lock of hair and insert it in a locket as a gift for a loved one.

Specialized books were published showing women how to create such work in this genre: sheaves of wheat finely embroidered on silk to bring happiness to a young newlywed, rings decorated with neoclassical urns, or lockets for a young mother carrying a lock of hair from each of her children. The creativity behind these items actually followed well-established codes.

Locks of hair from a departed loved one were placed in lockets, and rings were decorated with elegiac motifs set under glass. Hair was finely braided and twisted as works of art in such a way that would not be possible today. During the reign of Queen Victoria, especially after the death of Prince Albert, this "hairwork" style was very popular.

A Note

Jewelry made from hair (bracelets, chains, or rings especially) can be very irritating on bare skin.

Care and Maintenance

Rings and lockets with hair glued under the glass should not get wet: water will penetrate the setting, and the hair will slowly disintegrate!

A drop of lacquer will help set and place the shorter wisps on a chain or bracelet.

You can also use a wet mascara brush as a cleaning tool.

Wooden Charms

Since antiquity, talismans have been made out of wood to protect from the evil eye and from sickness. In the west, the crucifixion of Christ gave rise to a belief in wood as a source of protection. This is the origin of the expression "knock on wood" that makes reference to the Holy Cross; thousands of its fragments are kept in reliquaries.

The most celebrated talisman is the Talisman of Charlemagne; even the word "talisman" implies a function more secular and propitiatory than religious.

In England, the fashion for Victorian sentimental jewelry produced accessories in oak, the sacred wood of the Celts, often inlaid with silver or steel wire. The more precious woods such as dark ebony, spotted snakewood, or sandalwood were often used by jewelers, who were keen to use these resources, enriching them with semiprecious stones or

✳ Scented wood

To polish and perfume wooden jewelry, rub with a soft cloth moistened with several drops of sandalwood oil.

gold and silver studs. In India, rosary beads and bracelets have been shaped for ages from sandalwood, which is often engraved or sculpted. Upon contact with the skin, they exude a sweet odor.

CARE AND MAINTENANCE

Wood that is crafted into jewelry can become fragile. If it is placed in a dry atmosphere, it can crack. When dropped on a hard surface, it can break or split. To maintain its shiny and satiny polish, clean it with a cloth moistened with oil. Using the old-fashioned method of applying beeswax can be very effective (modern products contain silicones that can ruin some precious woods).

Do not wash your hands when you are wearing wooden rings and remember to avoid contact with water; this will certainly lead to splitting and cracks!

Chain link bracelet of sandalwood and silver, dating from the mid-twentieth century and signed by Boivin.

As black as ebony. A necklace by the Catalan Gemma Pixot, decorated with patinated bronze designs, placed next to rings set with jade and diamonds.

Glass and Crystal, Extremely Fragile

The invention of glass took place over many years. In his *Natural History*, Pliny the Elder was sure that it was discovered accidentally by Egyptian sailors who had made a fire on the beach with firewood propped up with blocks of saltpeter buried in the sand. From the effects of the heat, the saltpeter and the sand melted, producing a solid material like stone, which was brilliant and translucent. Thus glass was born. In any case, it is certain that the Egyptians used col- ored glass extensively to make beads and imitate precious stones. The use of glass beads has spread around the world over the centuries, but as a material, glass has been used sparingly due to its fragility.

RINGS AND BANGLES

Exceptions exist, of course, such as the "ouch" ring, sold in the nineteenth cen- tury at the fair of Beaucaire. This was a thin glass ring, decorated with streaks of color and worn sometimes on the knuckle, which young men offered to their fiancées or to the one they had promised themselves to for that day. It was because these rings easily broke from the least amount of shock and could cut the finger that they were given this name.

Poetic earrings of floral design, made in rocaille style. Carefully threaded onto bronze wire, these tiny beads allow the artist to be creative and rediscover the inspiration for beadwork from centuries past.

In India, for a long time, only married women were allowed to wear glass bangles (kanch-ki-choodi), which date back to 2700 BC. From the wrist to the elbow, the arm is covered in dozens of bracelets of different colors. As the women never take them off, the clinking sound signals their presence. The bracelets are fairly resistant except when they are separated. If they fall on a hard surface, they will break.

Adorning oneself in beads is a child's game that every young girl has played at some point. Young girls may pretend they are princesses for the day, putting together a set of jewelry to decorate their neck and hair. Some adults never lose their taste for such shimmering ornaments.

Modern Indian bracelets. Slowly but surely, synthetic materials are replacing traditional glass, but this change does not detract in any way from the colorful aesthetic of these dozens of bangles.

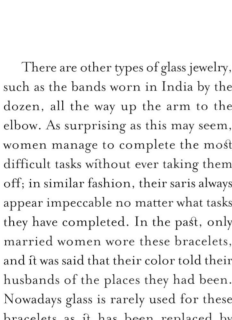

There are other types of glass jewelry, such as the bands worn in India by the dozen, all the way up the arm to the elbow. As surprising as this may seem, women manage to complete the most difficult tasks without ever taking them off; in similar fashion, their saris always appear impeccable no matter what tasks they have completed. In the past, only married women wore these bracelets, and it was said that their color told their husbands of the places they had been. Nowadays glass is rarely used for these bracelets as it has been replaced by plastic, which is lighter and unbreakable.

AN ANCIENT SKILL

In Venice, for centuries, artisans made bracelets, rings, and earrings from blown glass that bear colored inclusions or gold and silver powder.

Crystal glass should not be confused with the crystal mineral. It is, in fact, blown glass, whose name of Italian origin, *crystallo*, evokes the transparency of ice. The technique was invented by the Romans. It was later transferred to Asia before it came back to Venice and spread throughout Europe, especially among cutters in Bohemia and England.

Since the end of the seventeenth century, glassmakers have added lead oxide to make thicker, heavier crystal that can be cut and engraved.

In the seventeenth century, applying stonecutters' methods to cut glass, beautiful diamond imitations were created. These rhinestones were mounted on gold or silver, and the workmanship was superb.

Set of Napoleon III rock crystal jewelry. The transparent stones are faceted and capture light from the slightest movement.

On this antique cider carafe is a necklace made of uncut pieces of crystal that have never been touched by a stonecutter; next to it is another necklace with stones that have been faceted and then polished, giving them a fully transparent look.

In the nineteenth century, crystal was used to make necklaces of faceted beads, earrings that looked like drops of water—fashioned into fruit or floral shapes—or even large brooches inspired by the plant world. These were sometimes mounted in the same way as diamond tremblers, with elements that shook with the slightest movement of the wearer.

In the twentieth century, the famous crystal maker Lalique created a crystal ball that was so successful that it is still fabricated today and sold all over the world. The house of Baccarat also creates beautiful colored parures with a transparency and fineness that resemble precious stones.

Care and Maintenance

To prevent knocking or dropping it, glass jewelry should be easy to wear. But you must be very careful with it, storing the jewelry in a silk cloth, for example, and protecting it from any kind of shock.

Although less fragile than glass, crystal does not react well to shocks. Rings in particular break easily when they are exposed to the perils of everyday life.

Left

Scarab pinned to a straw hat. The color of the straw matches the colors of the enameled wings.

Right

To avoid losing a brooch from your clothing, try this tip: after piercing the material with the pin, thread it through an elastic band on the back side. Push the pin through to the front side of the material and clasp it.

✳ Over time

Because bronze contains copper and is fairly sensitive to oxidation, it may become spotted with verdigris.

Bronze, Thousands of Years Old

Included among the ornaments of ancient civilization are the works of the Celts, who originally populated northern Europe.

Their jewels—created in gold, silver, and bronze—exhibited great creativity. The bronze was an alloy of copper and pewter, to which silver was sometimes added. It was used often since gold was extremely expensive.

The torque—a stiff-neck ring that was twisted around the neck with the ends spread apart—was a characteristic Celtic ornament. Discovered in France, Celtic sepulchres dating from seventh century BC revealed a necropolis where men and women were buried in ceremonial garb. The women wore their jewels: torques that were sometimes adorned with coral and finely sculpted bracelets, fibulae (fasteners in the form of pins for clothes and veils), and earrings. One of these women was found wearing a special pendant at the end of a large chainmail necklace, an amulet representing a person with legs in the shape of a lyre.

In other parts of the world, such as Africa and India, bronze was used extensively in the making of jewelry for beads, necklaces, and bracelets worn on the wrist or ankle.

Neglected in Europe for centuries, bronze was rediscovered by jewelers at the beginning of the twentieth century.

CARE AND MAINTENANCE

Easy to live with, bronze is solid and resistant to shocks. Antique bronze jewelry does not need to be kept clean in order to maintain its patina.

Bronze can be cleaned with soap and water, but do not try to make it shiny. If it becomes lackluster, a little bit of lemon juice is sufficient to give it back its shine.

Left and right

This Baoulé African necklace is made of spherical bells and engraved designs, which were used in the past to weigh metal. The anemone is a creation of Claude Lalanne, as is the fuchsia necklace (right). This artist reinterprets nature and works in both bronze and galvanized copper. His jewelry expresses his talent, which is baroque as well as inventive, refined, and sensitive.

Jewelry from Around the World

Jewelry from faraway places fascinates us because it carries a history within it. «Whether they are trophy jewels, medicinal jewels, offerings, or seductions, they express the heritage of a culture, a social and ritual context, carrying a significance in the materials from which they are composed.» Natacha Wolters, *Les perles*, Éditions Syros, 1996.

The History of Beads

The term "bead" encompasses all kinds of precious stones as well as pierced objects of many kinds. From a seed to a pebble, from a bone to a shell, from a claw to a precious stone, including the meleagrine pearl, of course, each one is as beautiful as the next; the imagination of mankind is limitless in this domain.

Since antiquity, with the invention of glass, artisans have endeavored to make all sorts of beads in the most varied shapes, colors, and motifs. From the sepulchres of our ancestors, we have uncovered unsuspected trades that must have occurred from the dawn of civilization, in lands that were populated by nomads living off hunting and gathering. Glass beads, which have served as ornamentation since glass was discovered, were also used for trading. They were transported from Sumeria and

Egypt, across the desert of Afghanistan and into Mauritania. But, it was in Carthage that the craft of antique beads truly flourished. The Phoenicians perfected the most complex techniques, allowing them to create extraordinary beads in the shape of a head, eyes, mouth, hair, beard, or a turban of contrasting colors.

Fashioned by hand, antique beads were never perfect or regular. The holes for threading were usually very large. Sometimes the holes were not pierced evenly through the center, making them difficult to thread.

When assessing multicolored beads, with motifs, inspect them carefully: the colors should be visible on the inside of the bead, in layers of alternating colors. When the colors or motif appear only on the surface, the bead is not as old.

Left

An old Latin American sculpture is adorned, like a divinity, with necklaces from other continents. Around his neck rests a necklace made of glass and bronze openwork beads from Sudan. The yellow sautoir and the green necklaces were made with excavated glass beads probably from Mali, which were bought in Egypt. Between them lies a necklace with beads that were excavated in Afghanistan in the ancient Bactrian territories.

✳ Ancient clasps

These clasps (worn down and damaged), made by hand from unfinished materials, along with the date on the coin, help distinguish the antique necklaces from recent imitations of machine-made industrial glass.

A FORM OF PAYMENT

The beads from Venice or Bohemia were small stones scattered in various colonies by Europeans looking to mollify the local population. In exchange, they received ivory, gold, precious wood, and furs. Today, collectors treasure these beads—objects that were once considered cheap.

Beginning in the ninth century, Venice became the capital of the glass techniques that had been inherited from antiquity. Thousands of tons of beads emerged from Venetian workshops to find their way in the world. A universal currency, the small beads made their path across all the commercial routes. Trade beads are the most attractive and the most famous. Westerners (Dutch,

Spaniards, English, Portuguese, and French) purchased their slaves for their plantations in the New World from chieftains in Africa in exchange for a certain weight of these colored beads made in Venice, and later in Bohemia. To stock and transport them, the beads were threaded on a string that formed a sort of necklace in varying lengths and weights. Women in India wore these strings of beads as a necklace, joining them together with pieces of braided jute or raffia that are held together by a pierced attachment that acts as a sort of snap.

Above left and right
A necklace from Nagaland, a northern Indian state and a Zulu bracelet from South Africa. The glass beads from Venice and later from Bohemia used to be amassed and arranged into strands of varying lengths. In certain countries in Africa and Asia, women took over these colorful collections, twisting them into necklaces that were clasped together with a thick piece of hemp and a local coin that looked like a button.

Following page, left
Fish "caught" in Spain (the smallest), in Rajasthan (the largest), and in Lebanon. The fish has always been a symbol of fertility and luck and has served as protection against the evil eye.

Following page, right
Antique glass beads, excavated in Afghanistan. Rare and valuable, these beads were blown and decorated with colors and motifs taken from the earth.

Jewels from Africa

A land of migration and commerce, Africa is a continent that has been subjected to the influences of many foreign cultures. The ancient world, Byzantium, the Ottoman Empire, and Islam have left behind their customs and experiences as souvenirs in these lands. African jewelry is also an expression of a symbolic language, which is translated through the use of certain materials, colors, and distinct motifs.

While gold and precious stones often come from Africa, material value is not always the most important quality of their jewels. It is not rare to meet a Maasai warrior displaying rolls of used film or wearing safety pins covered in glass as earrings. Even colored copper or plastic wires used for electrical networks are gathered to make necklaces, bracelets, and earrings in styles that go back to ancient times.

For those who cannot afford gold, there are resins, terra-cotta covered in gold, or even more shocking, gold-plated straw called "Timbuktu gold." Solid bronze, brass, copper, and other metal alloys are also used, along with natural materials, such as ivory, wood, bone, horns, and elephant hair and skin.

Silverwork, enamel, and filigree are the specialties of the Maghreb, along with heavy amber necklaces and coral mixed with amulets or large enamel, and carved beads. In the past, young married women in the Maghreb would wear jewelry made of gold or a gold mix, together with beads pressed into a perfumed paste of ground rose petals, cloves, henna, and musk: the perfume was so strong that the scent still lingered on their jewelry many years later.

Left

People have perfected bead-weaving techniques on every continent and in all civilizations. Color choices are often symbolic.

Above right

Antique bracelet from Great Kabylie, Algeria, in silver, decorated with filigreed enamel and coral. The green, blue, and yellow enamel colors are characteristic of many pieces of Kabylie metalwork.

Previous page, left

Inexpensive jewelry made from silver-colored metal and colored glass is available in the Moroccan markets and bazaars.

Previous page, right

African necklace made of hand-decorated, dyed beads, placed on top of a Berber pitcher from southern Morocco.

Jewels from Asia

Lands of the fabulous jewels, this continent abounds in jewelry that reflects many diverse influences. Animism, totemism, and shamanism have marked the works of artisans over the centuries. Finely worked silver, enamel, filigree, and carvings dominate. The work is decorated with coral, cornelian, and turquoise, crafted in colors that protect and bring luck.

Jewelry in these lands was associated with magic, as it was believed that it could ward off illness, the evil eye, and bad spirits that roamed the region where life was constantly threatened by tribal warfare and extreme climate conditions.

✳ Patina

To distinguish antique jewels from those that are manufactured today, look them over for a while. The colors should seem less vivid, the contours of the metallic parts are usually worn down, and the patina of time shows its effects.

Jewels from the Americas

The great Amerindian civilizations have left their mark on the jewelry of both North and South America. Their primary materials were shells and stones (nephrite, jadeite, turquoise, and rock crystal). Workmanship in precious metals, gold, and silver came later, perfected by the pre-Colombian jewelers. They mastered the skills of melting wax, hammering metals, and embossing leather and they showed themselves to be remarkable lapidaries.

The Native Americans who lived in the Amazon forest used materials from their natural environment: feathers, seeds, and bronzed scarabs.

As for the Native Americans of North and Central America, the use of silver, jade, turquoise, and coral allowed them to make the type of jewelry celebrated by Frida Kahlo. Proud of her Mexican heritage, she appeared in voluminous layers of necklaces wherever she went,

Above

This pendant of woven beads comes from Afghanistan.

Right

Nepalese medicine necklace (worn for protection from sickness and bad luck) made of amulets: animal claws, beneficial stones, ancient coins, and ornamental seeds.

Following page, left

Frida Kahlo, a Mexican artist, loved to adorn herself in the jewelry and clothes of her native country. She often wore heavy Amerindian necklaces and silver jewelry, such as the filigree silver earrings shown here.

Following page, right

A Mexican necklace with milagros: ex-votos in silver-plated copper in the shape of an arm, leg, hand, heart, eyes, torso, and even a chicken.

along with her imposing earrings and bracelets, which she wore with traditional scarves, blouses, and skirts.

The Native Americans of New Mexico have long been famous for jewelry made of silver and stones, which employs a universal symbolism and magic and blends their native ancestral beliefs with the religion of the conquering Spaniards. From the time that tourism made its entry into their world, their workmanship has felt its impact: silver is now worked with industrial methods, and imitation stones are everywhere. The silver jewelry of yesteryear has become antique, such as the famous conches and leather belts decorated with large silver motifs in the shape of shells embedded with turquoise.

Age does not constitute the only criteria of quality. If you can feel the hand of the artisan in the work—and if it is a skilled one—it is irrelevant when the piece was made. Jewelry must always be acquired because you fall in love with it. Its beauty, appeal, and charm are what you pay for.

Bakelite
Synthetic resin, made from formaldehyde and phenol, invented in 1907 by the engineer Baekeland, who gave it his name.

Brilliant cut
A multiple faceted cut intended to maximize the amount of reflected light from the stone, usually a diamond. This cut was made popular in the seventeenth century.

Briolette cut
A pear- or drop-shaped cut, with facets all the way around the stone to reflect light.

Cabochon
A smooth, rounded stone without facets. This cut is reserved for stones with inclusions, particularly certain emeralds, star rubies, and sapphires. It highlights the stone's color rather than its luster.

Cacholong
A white and shiny opal that looks like porcelain. This stone is highly valued among contemporary jewelry designers.

Cameo
Stone, shell (called a shell cameo), volcanic lava, glass, or ceramic sculpted in relief.

Cannetille
Gold or silver twisted into spiral wires to form designs. While this technique is more popular in Asia, it was used by western jewelers at the beginning of the nineteenth century.

Carat/karat
The unit of measurement used to legally define the fineness of gold as well as the measurement used to designate the weight of precious stones.

Choker
A necklace with beads of the same diameter. When the beads are arranged in descending order of size, it is referred to as a "graduated" necklace.

Clip
The name used for earrings made for non-pierced ears that clip onto the earlobe. This term also refers to a clip brooch that was in style during the 1940s and 1950s.

Corozo
A vegetable material extracted from the nut of the ivory palm tree. It is used to make imitation ivory (vegetable ivory).

Coulas
This heavy, rigid bangle (made of silver or gold) closes with two large clasps and was worn by people from Arles, France. It is often adorned with a charm, usually the Maltese Cross.

Cowrie shell
A bivalve shell, with a shape that can look like a coffee bean or the female sex organ. A symbol of fortune and fertility, this small shell was used as a form of currency as well as a material from which to make African, Asian, and Oceanic jewelry.

Cross
There are all types of crosses. In France, most provinces had their own particular type of cross. The most popular style was the simple Jeanette. The Capucine and the Badine cross from the South and Provence contain cones of gold and silver that are sometimes embellished with diamonds, garnets, or other stones. The Boulonnaise, originally from Boulogne-sur-Mer is often ornamented with shells and fine filigree. In Normandy, crosses displayed cones of gold or silver or were ornamented with doves of gold, enamel, or citrine, while the handiwork on the cross of Rouen often looked like golden lace, adorned with diamonds or strass. The articulated Papillon cross gets its name from the sculpted and ribbed designs that surround the settings of stone or strass. The Maintenon, which is heavily ornamented, includes cone-shaped stones surrounded by a fine field of gold and silver filigree. The Maltese cross was favored in Arles, ornamented with black and white enamel.

Crystal
A type of white inclusion inside a diamond, which resembles a crack; it may be shaped like a feather or a plant.

Cushion cut
Old-fashioned cut for a stone creating the square or rectangular shape of a cushion that is rounded on the edges.

Doublet
A composite gem made from combining two layers that include a valuable stone or glass joined with another colored layer, used to strengthen or imitate the color of the stone. Doublets are most common for opals and emeralds.

Electrum
Alloy of silver or gold used in ancient times. Not to be confused with *elektron*, the ancient Greek word for amber.

Esclavage
Special "slave necklace" featuring medallions that may be either enameled or ornamented with colored glass, joined together with a multistrand chain choker with chains of different lengths. These were traditionally offered to a fiancée as a wedding gift in the late eighteenth and early nineteenth centuries.

Faith ring
The faith ring or promise ring is designed with two interlaced hands. It seals the relationship of an engaged couple. This type of ring has existed for hundreds of years.

Fetter chain
Chain made of links that are elongated, reminiscent of slave chains.

Fibula
A metal clasp, sometimes made of precious metal, that holds two parts of a garment together with a pin. Fibula existed in ancient times.

Filigree
Work composed of gold or silver wire that is interlaced and welded together.

Flaw
A term designating a defect in a diamond or other precious stone.

Galalith
This "milk stone" was invented in 1906 and is made of a milk protein called "casein" treated with formaldehyde. It is the ancestor of modern-day plastic. It looks like Bakelite and has been used to make costume jewelry and practical objects.

Gemstone
A precious material of mineral (precious and fine stones) or organic (pearls, amber, coral) origin used to decorate jewelry.

Glass painting
A painting is created directly under a piece of transparent glass. *Fixés églomisés* refer to the art of gilding motifs on the back of glass.

Gold Filled or *Doublé Or*
Method by which two pieces of gold or metal are fused together by pressure under heat. This technique was used in the nineteenth century but has been replaced by plating.

Grain
Unit of measurement used for the weight of a pearl.

Granulation
An antique goldsmith's technique whereby tiny metal balls were fused onto a surface of the same metal to decorate a piece of jewelry. Granulation was fashionable in the nineteenth century after Etruscan graves that contained magnificent golden jewels ornamented with granulation were uncovered.

Hallmark

The legal mark engraved on a piece of precious metal (platinum, gold, silver). The hallmark may be a number indicating the fineness of the metal (specific quantity): 750 parts of gold out of 1,000 for 18 karats, 484/1,000 for 14 karats, 375/1,000 for 9 karats; 925 for silver and 950 for platinum. It may also appear as a different symbol that varies by country: an eagle's head for France, for example. The goldsmith or jewelry designer may also stamp their distinctive mark.

Heating and other color-changing techniques

Heating was an old-fashioned technique used to change the color of a stone by placing it in an oven designed for that purpose. Later, radiation techniques were developed under which the stones are exposed to radium or X-rays. This method is most often used to darken the color of diamonds.

Inclusion

Irregularity in a stone. Perfectly pure stones are rare. Diamonds are the only stones that can be pure when viewed under a loupe at ten times magnification. Some inclusions actually add value when they are arranged in certain patterns, such as in star rubies, sapphires, or rutilated quartz, or even in the form of an insect in amber.

Intaglio

Design engraved onto a stone or into metal. The intaglio may serve as a seal or stamp.

Jardin

Inclusions inside an emerald. The French refer to the large number of inclusions as a "jardin" or garden.

Jaseron chain

Type of antique chain made with a series of fine links joined two by two.

Matte finish

Metal or silver that has been given a matte finish by removing the polish through brushing or dipping it in an acid bath.

Niello

Engraved or chiseled metal, inlaid with black enamel. Silver nielloware has long been popular with Russian metalsmiths.

Opal glass

Imitation opal made of vitreous material with a bluish milky tint. Opal glass may also be pink or jade green.

Orient

The term describing the luster of a pearl. The orient is due to the reflection of light on the layer of nacre that envelopes the pearl. *Essence d'orient* was a technique used in the eighteenth century to make imitation pearls using fish scales and animal glue.

Paillon

A thin sheet of metallic foil (silver or copper) placed under a stone to enhance its luster. Many stones were set with a paillon in the seventeenth, eighteenth, and nineteen century to give them more brilliance and sometimes to change or intensify their color.

Parure

A matched set of jewelry of the same style: necklace, bracelet, earrings, crown, hair comb, brooch, and buttons. A simple parure includes only a necklace and earrings or perhaps a brooch and earrings. The set is often presented in a leather box lined with velvet or satin.

Patina

Color created over time. Patina can also be created from artificial coloring added to a material.

Pendant

Jewel suspended from a chain, a velvet string, or leather cord.

Pendant bail

Name given to the piece that attaches a pendant or medallion.

Plating

Common metal covered with a thin layer of gold or silver.

Poissarde

Pendant earrings, designed with a geometric S pattern, which reinforces the clasp of these light, hanging precious metal (gold or silver) earrings. They were in style at the end of the eighteenth and beginning of the nineteenth centuries in France. Their name comes from the women who wore them originally—fisherwomen or wives of fishmongers—known for their coarse and garish attire.

Pomponne

Alloy of copper and zinc used to imitate gold. It was produced in the eighteenth century in the hôtel de Pomponne, from which it derives its name. The English equivalent is called Pinchbeck.

Rhinestone

The old name given to rock crystal as well as to nonmineral crystal stones (strass).

Rivière

Necklace or bracelet set in a continuous line of flowing gemstones. Diamonds in this arrangement were particularly appreciated in the eighteenth century for their natural and pure quality.

Rose cut

Antique diamond cut to look like a rosebud. The bottom of the diamond is flat, while the crown is faceted.

Sautoir

A long necklace or chain, worn in one or several strands. A watch on a long chain could sometimes be worn in sautoir style. Many years ago, the length and thickness of the chain reflected the size of its owner's fortune.

Setting

The way a stone is mounted. The setting may be pronged, which allows all the facets of the stone to be seen. With a closed setting, the cutlet and a portion of the stone are hidden.

Silk

Shimmering silklike inclusions, characteristic of sapphires and rubies.

Sleeper earrings

Earrings made of two hinged parts, embellished with diamonds or stones. They are constructed with a clasp that hooks the earring together. Sleepers were given their name as women can sleep with these earrings on, without fear of losing them.

Slide

A piece of metal jewelry with a design on it, pierced with an opening to allow for the insertion of a chain or ribbon. In the nineteenth century, slides were often heart-shaped, but they were also made in the shape of balls or were round-, rectangular-, square-, or sun-shaped.

Strass

Lead glass, used until the end of the eighteenth century to imitate precious stones. Colorless, it can imitate diamonds. When colored red, blue, or green, it imitates a ruby, sapphire, or emerald.

Studs

Small earrings with posts for inserting through pierced ears. They may be made of gold, pearls, stones, or diamonds.

Swan neck

Earring clasp in the form of a simple S shape. This makes the earring easy to insert, but also easy to lose, especially when wearing high necks or scarves. A small metal or plastic stopper may be slid over the wire to secure the earring behind the ear.

Vermeil

Silver covered with a layer of fine gold.

Water

An archaic word used to describe the clarity of a stone, as in "a diamond of the finest water."